# TAKE CHARGE OF YOUR CAREER

*A guide to organizing and conducting a successful job search in these competitive times.*

## MARY ANN CHIMERA

Take Charge of Your Career: A guide to organizing and conducting a successful job search in these competitive times.
Copyright © 2023 by Mary Ann Chimera

Published in the United States of America
ISBN   Paperback:        979-8-89091-391-3
ISBN   eBook:            979-8-89091-392-0

All rights reserved. No part of this publication may be reproduced, stored in a retrieval system or transmitted in any way by any means, electronic, mechanical, photocopy, recording or otherwise without the prior permission of the author except as provided by USA copyright law.

The opinions expressed by the author are not necessarily those of ReadersMagnet, LLC.

ReadersMagnet, LLC
10620 Treena Street, Suite 230 | San Diego, California, 92131 USA
1.619. 354. 2643 | www.readersmagnet.com

Book design copyright © 2023 by ReadersMagnet, LLC. All rights reserved.

Cover design by Tifanny Curaza
Interior design by Don De Guzman

Dedicated to my good friend,
Sue Steinmetz,
who continually inspires with her courage
and who first saw the possibility of a book
in my teaching and counsel.

# CONTENTS

INTRODUCTION: THE TAKE-CHARGE APPROACH TO CAREER MANAGEMENT ................................................................................................. 1

    The Passive Approach ............................................................................. 4
    Are you ready for changes? .................................................................... 5
    The TAKE-CHARGE Approach to Career Management ..................... 6
    The layout of this book ........................................................................... 7
    How this book came to be ..................................................................... 8

SECTION A: PREPARING FOR YOUR JOB SEARCH ................................. 10

    WHAT IS A RESUME? DO I REALLY NEED ONE? .......................... 11
        A resume is a sales document, an advertisement for you! ................. 11
        A resume is the first and perhaps the ONLY impression you will make on a prospective employer! ......................................................... 12
        A resume is a sampler of your qualifications and experience ........... 12
        For the employer, a resume is a REJECTION TOOL! ..................... 13
        A resume is a tool for organizing your job search! ............................ 15
        How long should a resume be? ............................................................ 15
        How about using a resume preparation specialist? ............................ 16

    ASSESSING YOUR QUALIFICATIONS .................................................. 18
        What kind of a job interests you? ....................................................... 19
        What was your job experience? .......................................................... 20
        Your education ...................................................................................... 22
        Your licenses and certificates ............................................................... 22
        Your job-related hobbies and memberships ...................................... 22
        Your know-how .................................................................................... 23
        What are your best qualities? .............................................................. 24

    PUTTING IT TOGETHER: INTRODUCING THE HIGH-IMPACT RESUME ................................................................................................... 25
        What information goes into a resume? ............................................... 26
        The STANDARD resume formats ..................................................... 26
        Introducing the HIGH-IMPACT Resume ........................................ 28
            Heading ........................................................................................... 28

    The Situation Wanted Ad for YOU .................................................................29
    The body of the Resume .................................................................................33
    Hands-On Knowledge ...................................................................................34
    Your experience ..............................................................................................34
    Your Education ..............................................................................................40
    Other possible entries ....................................................................................40
    Omit these entries .........................................................................................41
    Final touches .................................................................................................42

## WHAT ABOUT A COVER LETTER? ..............................................................43
## The HIGH-IMPACT Cover Letter ...................................................................45
    The body of the letter ....................................................................................46
    The Connection Maker ..................................................................................47
    The Back-Up ..................................................................................................49
    The Invite .......................................................................................................50

# SECTION B: SOLVING SPECIAL PROBLEMS ..................................................51

## LANDING THAT FIRST JOB ..............................................................................52
    Assessing your qualifications .........................................................................53
    Relevant work experience .............................................................................54
    Other relevant experience .............................................................................54
    The entry-level HIGH-IMPACT Resume .....................................................55

## CHANGING CAREERS .......................................................................................56
    Identifying needed skills ................................................................................57
    Moving up into Management .......................................................................57
    Identifying these skills in your work history ................................................58
    Preparing your HIGH IMPACT Resume .....................................................58

## BEATING AGE DISCRIMINATION .................................................................60
## OH! OH! YOU WERE FIRED! WHAT TO DO? WHAT TO DO? ..................63
    What really happened to you? ......................................................................63
    What to do? Assess your situation! ...............................................................64
    What to do? Devise a strategy ......................................................................66
    That crucial interview ...................................................................................69

# SECTION C: SAMPLE RESUMES & COVER LETTERS ....................................70

# SECTION D: CARRYING OUT YOUR JOB SEARCH .................................................. 88

## ORGANIZING YOUR JOB SEARCH: WHERE TO LOOK .......................... 89
- Working your network ................................................................. 89
- Headhunters ................................................................................ 90
- Professional conventions and job fairs ........................................... 92
- Advertising .................................................................................. 92
- National Media ............................................................................ 93
- Specialized Professional Publications ............................................. 94
- The Internet ................................................................................. 94
- Regional Media ............................................................................ 94
- Local Media ................................................................................. 94

## ORGANIZING YOUR JOB SEARCH: HOW TO LOOK ............................ 95
- Identifying and contacting potential employers ............................. 95
- Work your network ..................................................................... 97
- Check job postings ...................................................................... 97
- Attend conventions & job fairs .................................................... 97
- Working through headhunters ..................................................... 98
- Answering ads ............................................................................ 100
- Creating your own job and other over-the-transom approaches ..... 102

## QUALIFYING EMPLOYERS ..................................................................... 104
- Stability of the business ............................................................. 106
- Workplace environment ............................................................. 107

## THAT ALL-IMPORTANT INTERVIEW .................................................... 110
- The application form ................................................................. 111
- Three kinds of interview ............................................................ 113
- Negotiating your interview ........................................................ 113
- Negotiating terms of employment .............................................. 116

# INTRODUCTION

## THE *TAKE-CHARGE APPROACH* TO CAREER MANAGEMENT

# THE *TAKE-CHARGE APPROACH* TO CAREER MANAGEMENT

***YOU ARE IN CHARGE OF YOUR CAREER!*** Helping you to take advantage of that fact is the basis of the **TAKE-CHARGE APPROACH *to Career Management*** spelled out in these chapters.

The ***TAKE-CHARGE Approach*** is rooted in modern personnel administration practice widely used in the business world. It takes into account at every step those factors employers consider as they make recruiting, interviewing and hiring decisions. These employer concerns form the basis for the job search strategies presented in these pages.

By taking employer thinking into account, the ***TAKE-CHARGE Approach*** shows you how to present yourself to an employer in a way that makes your qualifications stand out from those of all other applicants whose resumes cross her desk. At the same time, the ***TAKE-CHARGE Approach*** helps you avoid common pitfalls preventing your qualifications and potential from ever being seriously considered by the very employer who needs your skills.

The ***TAKE-CHARGE Approach*** is also rooted in my experience in assisting hundreds of clients to forward their careers through enlightened job search strategies through preparing their resumes, providing information and conducting seminars. The ***TAKE-CHARGE Approach*** is a detailed roadmap for your quest to get into that satisfying job of your dreams, the job that draws on and develops your special talents, a position in which you can be productive.

You may have never considered that ***YOU** and only you* are the one in charge of your career and you may not fully believe it. Throughout a career, many circumstances come up – over which you have no control – to push you in one direction of another.

The economy goes through fat and lean years making jobs plentiful or scarce. You come out of college only to find few job openings in your field that particular year. Your company makes decisions about its future, impacting or changing your job status or description, sometimes drastically by putting you out of work. Someone else gets or is hired in for the promotion you thought was yours. You suddenly find yourself laid off or forced into early retirement.

Other people, opportunities which arise or you seek out, the firms you choose to work for and the socioeconomic climate of the times most certainly influence the direction your career takes over the forty to sixty years or more you're active in the workforce. Nevertheless, ***YOU*** decide just what you do for a living, where you do it and how long you do it.

That means at virtually any point in your career, it's up to *YOU* to manage your career, No one else has your interests fully at heart. You manage your career in part by making decisions whether to stay where you are or to seek out and take advantage of the range of other available opportunities.

Be assured that no matter how bleak the economy may look at any given moment, there is always a range of opportunities available to you! You may find unexpected opportunities even within your present place of employment.

Decisions about what you do with your working life and how you apply your talents to make a career for yourself are among the most important you will ever make. Over a lifetime, you will spend a substantial part of your time in the work setting you have chosen doing what you've chosen to do. Your life's work will substantially change your ideas and even define who you are and what you are about.

The old shibboleth holds true here. *Not to decide is to decide!* By not actively looking into change possibilities, you effectively opt to remain with your present job, no matter how unsatisfactory it is for you! This could be a much more costly decision than you realize in terms of what you might have accomplished and the impact that has on your life and health.

*YOU* alone know for certain at any point in your working life what your aspirations, dreams and job satisfaction requirements are. Only *YOU* care enough about the conditions you work under and the satisfaction you gain from your work to want to make changes. These simple facts put it squarely up to *YOU* to determine the course your career takes throughout your working life in order to ensure that your requirements are met.

You can choose to take a proactive or a passive approach to making career decisions. You can opt to ***TAKE CHARGE of your career*** or you can just let a career – a career with many features you don't like — happen to you, effectively handing charge of your career to circumstances or other people.

Should you choose to be proactive, these chapters will show you an approach that works. But first, we'll look at one that usually doesn't.

# *The Passive Approach*

So many people passively and unnecessarily allow other people and circumstances to make career choices for them! So often, they believe in their heart of hearts that jobs are scarcer than they really are both in good times and bad. Some have an unshakeable notion that they don't have what it takes to succeed in a challenging job.

Some just don't know what to do to find the right job for themselves. With low self-confidence and low expectations, they take little time to consider where they are going with their career. Consequently, they take the very first job offered whether it's a good match for their talents and desires, or not.

Only too often, they drift in an unsuitable job, putting in time and collecting a paycheck without making any attempt to move either themselves or the business forward. By so doing, they allow — even force — employers to make career decisions for them.

Given the law of averages, a passive approach to career management occasionally somehow works quite well for some few people. These fortunate few miraculously happen to land in jobs perfect for them with prospects they like, for which they have an aptitude with sympathetic employers who mentor them to a long productive, successful career.

Throughout these pages, we'll be pointing out that there are no hard and fast rules in the career management arena that apply absolutely and universally in every situation. Many people get and hold jobs and even find success against the odds by the sure luck of being in the right place at the right time with the right employer. Nevertheless, the odds say that you're much more likely to find success with proven career management strategies.

Typically, the outcome you want just doesn't happen with passive approaches. For far too many passive people, the match between the jobholder with her unique abilities, interests and expectations and the job and employer expectations is very poor or simply doesn't exist.

Far too often, a passive jobholder winds up in a workplace with a most unfortunate, even nonexistent, climate for personal growth or advancement. This creates a situation that further undermines a faltering self-esteem.

Persistent job dissatisfaction gives rise to workplace disruptions. Personalities clash. As employer expectations become increasingly unrealistic in regard to this worker, both employer and worker become more and more frustrated and lose hope.

At the least, employer expectations are out of sync with this jobholder's abilities and aspirations. Consequently, worker motivation to put effort into doing the job falls off sharply as a worker who has given up on herself flounders through a career.

The personal price paid for career passivity is high. Job dissatisfaction and the death of hope it brings about contribute substantially to psychological, social and medical problems, not only for the worker, but for those with whom she associates on and off the job.

This situation has repercussions for the employer as well. All the frustration of attempting to deal with an unmotivated, highly frustrated worker in the wrong job, the disturbances she creates in the workplace and the impact on the bottom line fall directly into his lap. Trying to find workable remedies distract him from important business concerns.

## *Are you ready for changes?*

Is your career going nowhere? Here are some questions to ask yourself:

- ✓ Is the work you're doing becoming more and more routine, boring and no longer challenging? Are there few opportunities to advance your career the way you want it to go in your current place of employment? Do you feel more and more bored, blocked and stagnant?

- ✓ Are you currently in an unfortunate, discouraging job situation? Do you find yourself reluctant to get up to go to work in the morning and in a hurry to leave at night? Do you spend your time at work thinking about evenings and weekends when you can get involved in what you really like to do?

- ✓ Are your firm's or your boss's employee policies and attitudes negative and unfavorable, even hostile toward all their workers or especially toward *you*?

- ✓ Are there other conditions in your workplace, unnecessary to the line of work you do, that constantly bug you, leaving you in a state of constant irritation and agitation or with feelings of despair or hopelessness?

If more than one or two of these conditions consistently apply, **why are you staying there?** It's high time to seek out and consider other opportunities. It's time to look into the ***TAKE-CHARGE Approach to Career Management!***

Don't quit your job just yet! Wait at least until you have job offers in hand. Take the time to acquaint yourself with the ***TAKE-CHARGE Approach.*** Then, establish a plan of action and carry it out.

It's an established truism that it's much easier to get a job while you still have one! Employers tend to believe that there's got to be something wrong with an applicant who's not currently employed, no matter what circumstances put him there.

The ***TAKE-CHARGE Approach to Career Management*** laid out in some detail in three SECTIONS of this book has proved itself highly effective for many people in making positive career moves.

# The TAKE-CHARGE Approach to Career Management

The *TAKE-CHARGE Approach* centers on concerns as both employee and active contributor to your employer's success. As a worker, you're much more likely to be productive in a positive environment attuned to your working style, doing projects you enjoy.

This approach is dedicated to helping you get there. Its further purpose is to put you on a positive career track, even to jump-start your career. You have rights to these things!

The *TAKE-CHARGE Approach* takes employer concerns into account as well, recognizing that you have a stake in the success of your employer's enterprise. Without that success, it is much more difficult for you to succeed. In turn, employers are served best by proactive thinking employees who have taken charge of their careers. Your employer has a stake in your success.

Highly successful careers come about through collaboration between employer and employee working together toward compatible goals. Working diligently toward the success of the enterprise that employs you is insurance for your own success.

Your employer has a right to the level of job performance and productivity she is paying you for. She and your coworkers have a right to a peaceful, non-disruptive workplace environment. She and they have a right to your compliance with reasonable workplace rules and standards.

The *TAKE-CHARGE Approach* is rooted in making substantial preparation as spelled out in **SECTION A**, following, before beginning any actual job-hunting. Preparation starts with taking time to determine in just what employment you truly want to invest your career from this point forward. That may or may not be your current field.

Your preparation begins with drawing up a *HIGH-IMPACT Resume* in a format, developed by the author, which has proved itself highly effective for many, many clients.

The *HIGH-IMPACT* format is designed to present your unique qualifications in terms of precisely what employers look for in making hiring decisions. Because it differs significantly from virtually all other resumes sitting on the employer's desk, your *HIGH-IMPACT Resume* is virtually guaranteed to draw attention to your qualifications.

The process discussed in SECTION A of this manual helps you to identify your assets for an employer, emphasizing those assets employers most value in language employers relate to. It takes into account how employers go about the hiring process.

Preparing your *HIGH-IMPACT Resume* guides you to understand and address more fully employer needs and viewpoints. The kind of thinking involved simultaneously readies you for later successful employer interviews and negotiations.

The ***TAKE-CHARGE Approach*** also draws on principles of successful sales technique. There are strong parallels between a successful sales campaign and a successful job search. In sales, the representative presents the advantages of a product or service to prospective buyers. The "product" you hope to present prospective employers is your services and expertise.

# *The layout of this book*

The *Take-Charge* preparation process is presented in the four chapters of SECTION A, fittingly titled ***Preparing for your job search***. First, we consider what a resume is, what it is not and what it is ideally supposed to do, along with some misconceptions of what it is and its purpose.

Misunderstanding your resume's purpose all too often is an extremely costly error leading to yours landing in a resume reviewer's reject pile. Poorly prepared resumes are a leading cause of job applicant disqualification. Without a clear understanding of what you are doing and why, you are very likely to include information that disqualifies you for the job you want and to omit information that qualifies you for it.

Next, we look at how long a resume should be, followed by consideration of choosing and using the services of a professional resume preparation specialist.

The second chapter shows how to assess your qualifications in language an employer relates to. The third introduces the ***HIGH-IMPACT Resume***, explains how it differs from the standard approach, and shows you, section by section, just how to put your information into the ***HIGH-IMPACT*** format.

The final chapter of SECTION A is a discussion of the advantages of using a cover letter while it introduces and lays out the format of the ***HIGH-IMPACT Cover Letter***, again, in some detail.

SECTION B, ***Solutions for Special Career Management Problems***, discusses modifications of the ***HIGH-IMPACT Resume*** and the job search process for four common situations faced by job seekers: landing that first job, changing careers, beating age discrimination and landing another job after being fired.

SECTION C features a varied group of sample resumes and cover letters prepared following the guidelines presented in SECTION A and SECTION B.

SECTION D, ***Carrying out your job search***, takes you into the active search phase of the ***TAKE-CHARGE Approach***. ***Where to look*** is discussed in terms of where employers are looking for qualified job applicants. ***How to look*** shows you how to put yourself together with an employer seeking to hire.

***Qualifying employers*** is a most important feature of the ***TAKE-CHARGE Approach***. It is one of several features which differentiate this approach from so many others, all of which focus exclusively on how to meet employer expectations. ***Qualifying employers*** is the process that takes into account *your* hopes and dreams, as well as what the employer offers in terms of job security, environment and favorable employee policies. By ***qualifying*** prospective employers, you insure that you actually get into a job situation leading to maximum personal job satisfaction as well as meeting the expectations of your next employer.

The final chapter of SECTION D — and the book — takes you through strategies for interviewing and negotiating with employers for the job you want. At this point, your hard work has paid off. You've found the right employer for you and you know how to talk to him to get the job of your dreams.

Scattered throughout SECTIONS A, B and D are ***HIGH IMPACT TIPS.*** Either they describe strategies that give you an edge over your competition or they guide you to avoid those pitfalls which trip up so many job seekers and disqualify them from further employer consideration.

# How this book came to be

Many strands in the author's background contribute to the know-how laid out in these pages.

With a degree in physics and graduate studies in engineering analysis, I was employed as an engineering analyst by two major firms for some fifteen years.

My years of working in industry have given me a strong sense of the real world of work. My own job searches have added a sense of the dilemma faced by unsophisticated job searchers facing the great unknown. That unsophisticated job hunter was me! Knowledge of the strategies of this book would have been so helpful back then!

Purely by chance while working as an engineer, I encountered graphology. As time went by, I became totally intrigued and began serious study of this means of interpreting the class of habitual behaviors we call "handwriting," in terms of what they reveal about individual personalities. As we do with all other human behaviors, we continually express our personalities through our handwriting.

This life-changing encounter led to lifelong fascination with the study of the vast variety of personalities as revealed in handwriting. As I applied what I was learning, I discovered how very different each of us is from every other individual.

Based on both my own experiences in various job assignments and observations of others in their job situations, I came to the conclusion that job satisfaction is rooted largely in fitting the job to the personality of the person in it. To broaden my insights into this question, I began to look especially at the question of placing people in jobs based on their personality characteristics.

To be more effective at this I began to study jobs as such in the hope of assisting clients to choose the career most suitable to their personalities to broaden my knowledge of job and the personnel field, I earned a certificate in personnel administration from New York University. There, I had the privilege of studying with some of the top people in the field, those experts who act as consultants to various firms throughout the country.

My fascination with personality then led to three years of clinical training in transactional analysis and gestalt therapy psychotherapy. Several years later, it led to the study of hypnosis and qualification as a hypnotherapist.

My duties as an engineer, reflecting my natural aptitudes, included technical writing and editing. I became a specialist in the documentation of engineering studies. Somewhat later, I wrote for, edited and published a small technical magazine for professional graphologists, called ***IMPACT Magazine.***

This enabled and provided discipline for conducting and presenting my and other graphologists' research into graphologists' questions and interpretations. To meet a bimonthly schedule, I had deadlines to meet and pages to fill. This intense effort disciplined and improved my writing skills and broadened my understanding of personality.

Returning to Ohio, I put these several threads of experience and technique to work with a small business called ***IMPACT Enterprises***. Under that name, I offer a variety of services, including resume preparation.

Clients frequently tell me employers find my clients' ***HIGH-IMPACT Resumes*** impressive. I've had referrals for my services from the state employment service.

In preparing resumes for my clients, my goal is to help them develop a presentation package that highlights their assets as potential contributors to the success of each firm they approach for employment. Drawing on my engineering systems analysis skills along with what I've learned from broad reading about promotion, marketing and layout while marketing my magazine and various handwriting services, I very quickly found that the traditional standard resume formats just didn't do the job on the level I sought to provide to my clients.

My resume preparation begins with a consultation with the client in which we explore his background and qualifications. This is very much like the interview he will subsequently have with the employer. As we talk, I am able to observe how he presents himself and what he says. Many ***HIGH-IMPACT TIPS*** in this book are based on these observations.

"Nobody knows this stuff! You ought to write a book!" one of my students exclaimed. That planted the seed that eventually became the book in your hands.

# SECTION A

## PREPARING FOR YOUR JOB SEARCH

# WHAT IS A RESUME? DO I REALLY NEED ONE?

Understanding what you are setting out to do in writing your resume helps you to prepare an effective one which accomplishes its purpose in getting you an interview. More important, preparing a resume with its purposes in mind helps you to focus your job search to get the job you really want which will advance your career.

So, just what is a resume supposed to accomplish for you? First let's look at what a resume is ***NOT!*** This will help you avoid common errors ending with your resume in the employer's round file.

- A resume is ***NOT*** your life's history!
- A resume is ***NOT*** even your career history!
- A resume is ***NOT*** simply a list of your previous employers!
- A resume is ***NOT*** a list of your vital statistics (age, sex, marital status and the like)!
- A resume is ***NOT*** a summary of your interests and achievements!

## A resume is a sales document, an advertisement for you!

An effective resume induces the employer to start thinking about not just whether you are employable but exactly where you'd fit into his operations in terms of what contribution you are likely to make to his bottom line.

To get a job, usually you have to make the opportunity to talk over with a prospective employer just where you will fit into his staff and how you can help him accomplish his business objectives. (I say "usually" because there are no absolutes in job searching.)

People get jobs in many, many ways, sometimes with no job search, no resume, no interview. This book is intended for everybody else. It also may serve to put you on the alert for any opportunities coming your way.

***THE FOREMOST PURPOSE OF A RESUME IS TO PERSUADE A PROSPECTIVE EMPLOYER TO TALK TO YOU ABOUT A JOB HE HAS IN MIND FOR YOU!*** A resume that gets you interviews for jobs with the potential for taking your career in the direction you want to go is an effective resume! It has done the job it was designed to do! Making the favorable impression once you've gotten the interview to land the job is up to you, not to your resume.

## Do you really need a resume?

When you have connections or a highly sought-after skill or a broad reputation for high quality performance or a potential employer takes a shine to you, probably not! Some people simply fall into superb career-advancing jobs simply by being in the right place at the right time.

The rest of us need resumes! Many employers simply won't talk to you until they have reviewed your resume. A well-crafted resume is an investment in your career success.

## A resume is the first and perhaps the ONLY impression you will make on a prospective employer!

Your resume may be your only opportunity to direct a prospective employer's attention to your qualifications and credentials.

An informative, well-organized and well-presented resume tells the prospective employer that you are a well-qualified class act. It tells her that you've taken time to do the research and to take her concerns into account.

A carelessly prepared and poorly presented resume says the opposite about you.

## A resume is a sampler of your qualifications and experience

Just what does the employer want to learn about you from your resume? She wants to know if and how your know-how and experience fit the job she wants to fill. She wants to know what there is in your background to build on in this new position for you. Your resume should tell enough to persuade her that it's worth her while to talk to you.

Think about the last time a salesman called on you. What did he do to persuade you to place an order?

My guess is that he laid out a sampling or did a demonstration of his wares. Your resume, standing in for you as your sales agent, should present a sample of your know-how and experience in a similar fashion to your prospective employer.

Just as the salesman does not give you the whole product, you need not necessarily give your employer every detail of your background and experience. You need just enough to arouse her interest in talking to you about what you have to offer her enterprise.

## *For the employer, a resume is a REJECTION TOOL!*

For the moment, put yourself in the shoes of a potential employer! You have expanded your business and want to hire five new people, three of them with highly specialized skills. You have posted the positions for your employees, put on an ad campaign, contacted employment agencies, put out the word with your friends, and taken all the usual steps to recruit new employees.

Whatever you did must have succeeded because now you have a stack of 450 resumes of people who want those five jobs.

What will you do? Interview 450 people? Obviously not! You have a business to run! That has to be your first priority! If you don't stay solvent, you won't be working yourself! Interviewing all those folks will take a lot of your time, or your staff's time: time you have to pay for in salaries, time they won't be spending on performing their ordinary duties. It's just not economically feasible, especially when many of those 450 potential employees are unsuited and unqualified for any of your five new positions.

So, with a large company, you will have someone from your personnel department look through the pile of resumes in order to narrow down the pool of candidates to a more manageable number. Usually, that comprises the three or five most desirable candidates for each position based on the information provided in and with their resumes. In a smaller enterprise, as owner or manager, you'll carry through the following steps yourself.

Resume reading is an art. Courses are taught on just what to look for in order to eliminate potentially undesirable employees. Examples are people likely to cause problems in the workplace and those unlikely to remain in the job long enough to produce after recouping the employer's investment in hiring them.

There are considerable costs in hiring and training new employees to the job and company procedures. These are estimated to be at least twice the employee's annual salary in addition to that salary. One rule of thumb is that an employee must remain at least two years before becoming an asset to the company.

A resume reviewer may go through the pile of resumes three or four times before coming up with his recommendations for interviews. With each pass, a group of resumes is eliminated.

First to go are sloppy, glaringly poorly crafted resumes: those with poor presentation, misspelled words, several obvious typos and the like. When an applicant doesn't care enough or isn't smart enough to turn in a presentable resume, that often translates into a slovenly appearance and slovenly job performance. Also gone on the first pass are those whose backgrounds are manifestly unsuitable to the jobs in question, at least in the eyes of the resume reviewer.

On the next pass, the resume reviewer does detective work. What's wrong with this candidate? A resume showing too many jobs, especially over a short period of time, will be eliminated. A candidate with six different jobs in five years is likely to be a job hopper with loyalty to neither job nor employer (therefore a poor risk), have a poor attitude leading to problems with employer or colleagues, or have a poor work ethic. Any of these may have led to her being dumped by previous employers.

Is something being covered over? An indicator of this and other potential problems is unexplained gaps in dates of employment, long periods of not working. Is this a resume of a person over or nearing 40 years of age? Age discrimination usually occurs at this stage of the process where it is impossible to detect. Often, resumes raise red flags that the applicant may not be aware of. We'll discuss all of these as we go along in later chapters.

Only on the next go-rounds does the resume reviewer begin actively to look for the most qualified candidates. However, it's not unlikely for standout resumes to be set apart right from the start for further review. The resume reviewer ranks, say, the top ten candidates for each position. To do this, he takes a good look at the stated qualifications of each applicant with respect to the requirements of each of the five open positions. Next, he forwards his top five choices for each position to the interviewer or team of interviewers who will do the actual hiring, holding the next five most desirable resumes in reserve.

In a large corporation, copies of these five most desirable resumes typically are given to a team of three or more people including the person who will manage the applicant eventually hired, that manager's boss and an interview specialist from the personnel department. The team may also include a technical specialist from the department in which the candidate will eventually work. Each of these will review the resumes once again, with an eye to eliminating still more applicants whose qualifications do not match job requirements.

Those applicants whose resumes survive are contacted and interviewed. Should none be hired, the process is repeated with the next five most desirable applicants.

***AN EFFECTIVE RESUME SURVIVES THE ELIMINATION PROCESS!*** It puts you on the short list of those who will be interviewed. Of course, you want your resume to be one of the standouts set aside for review from the beginning of the process. Taking the time to create a quality resume will put yours there!

## *A resume is a tool for organizing your job search!*

Building an effective resume revolves around researching what assets you have that make you attractive as a potential employee in a job that both interests you and advances your career. This is precisely the information you need at your fingertips for an effective job search. Your research and the process of presentation also prepare you for interviews with prospective employers.

Good sales technique begins with knowledge of a product's selling points. In a job search, *YOU* with your skills, experience and attitude, are the "product" you are marketing. The process of preparing an effective resume helps you to think through your background in order to identify your selling points.

Even if you think you don't need a resume, going through the process of preparing one will better equip you, not just for the rest of your job search process, but for advancing your career. It is very likely that you will discover personal career assets and/or goals that you did not realize you had. You may even find yourself making a career change and so looking for a different type of job than you had in mind originally.

There are endless possibilities for someone with your precise background, abilities and interests. Taking the time to identify your assets may be the best investment you can make in managing your career.

## *How long should a resume be?*

Put it this way: In working for hundreds of clients, I have never prepared a resume of more than *ONE PAGE* in length. An amazing amount of information can be contained in a single page. When coming up short on space on one page, look over the information to see how it can be condensed or what can be safely eliminated to bring it back down to a single page.

Executives and resume reviewers are generally busy people. With their other duties, they don't have the time and are unwilling to use what time they have to go through mountains of excess verbiage. An overly long resume strongly suggests either that you are very impressed with yourself or a long-winded inefficient boor or maybe both! It further suggests inconsideration of your prospective employer's time. For them, this translates into inconsiderateness in other matters.

Go back a few pages to the description of resume screening. Consider the resume reviewer's dilemma. Once again, you have a pile of 450 resumes to go through on your desk and other work to do after that job. How much time are you going to devote to reading a seven-page opus?

Two-page resumes have been known to make it through the screening process. You might squeak by with two full pages with extraordinary qualifications or an inexperienced resume reviewer. As the length of the resume increases, the probability of the resume being "filed" increases exponentially.

A one-page resume packed with information suggests that you are efficient, are considerate of your potential employer and know how to organize your information. That has to be a plus for you.

## How about using a resume preparation specialist?

A competent resume preparation specialist is worth his weight in gold. He can help you sort out your background and skills for what is useful and focus your resume on the job you want. His interview is a useful rehearsal and preview for interviews to come with prospective employers. He can educate you on how to approach potential employers, evaluate the way you present yourself, pick up on those habits, mannerisms and phrasings you may not be aware of which make an unfavorable impression on employers and recommend changes.

The problem is finding a competent resume preparation specialist! Resume writing is a poorly defined field with no certifying agencies. One must rely on one's instincts, investigative skills and common sense to find a competent resume preparation specialist.

Anyone can advertise resume preparation services. It takes only an ad in the paper. A lot of folks see it as a quick way to make money. Their only qualifications may be typing skills or a computer program. What you get from them may be beautifully typed and have good graphics, but that is essentially all. The content may be anything at all and may be totally ineffective in putting your qualifications in front of an employer.

Among my collection of resumes provided to me by clients are several prepared by people who style themselves as "professional" resume preparation specialists. One, a two-pager, consists of names and addresses of former employers, nothing more! What would happen to such a resume? My guess is that it would go immediately into the round file.

Be particularly wary of those agencies that assign preparation of your resume to a secretary or typist. Do they ask for sufficient information for an effective resume? Or do they simply ask for a list of previous employers? If the latter, don't waste your time or money on letting them prepare one for you, even if it is at no cost to you.

How do you know that a resume preparation specialist is competent? Ask questions! What is in his background to qualify him as an expert? A background in personnel or, at least, experience with reviewing resumes is ideal. Ask to see examples of the product. What do his resumes look like? What kind of information do they contain? If you were a resume reviewer, what kind of impression would they make on you?

In working with a resume preparation specialist, keep in mind that it is **YOUR** resume that is being prepared, not his! He is responsible for providing you with a clean error-free copy. **YOU** are ultimately responsible for its content. **YOU** are the authority on the accuracy of the information provided.

Take time to review the completed resume thoroughly. Carefully scan it for errors. Take it home and read it through again at your leisure. Make sure that all information is correct. If corrections need to be made, return the resume to the preparation specialist. If he has sound reasons for not making those changes, he will discuss those with you. The final decision is still yours.

# ASSESSING YOUR QUALIFICATIONS

Now comes the fun part of your job search, the part that lays the groundwork for everything else you will do in your job search process: figuring out just what you want to do with your career and just what you have to offer makes the whole process of career management much easier.

Grab a few sheets of blank paper and something to write with. As we move through this chapter, walk with me through the process of assessing just what you have to offer an employer. We're going to pull out of you what your selling points are so you can design an effective personalized resume that takes you where you want to go.

Better still, find a partner who is willing to go through the process with you. Ask each other the questions laid out as each of you observes your partner as she responds. That way, each of you may pick up on something that the other is saying or doing that either of you'd miss going through the process by yourself.

This walk-through is designed to give you the words and phrases needed to craft a unique, personalized and effective resume — a resume that grabs the attention of prospective employers. It is modeled on my interview with a client designed to come up with the information I need to prepare an effective resume for him.

In those **HIGH-IMPACT Resumes** I prepare for clients, I make a point of using as much of their own language to describe themselves, their goals, experience and qualifications as I can. After all, each resume is crafted to speak for *YOU* to prospective employers.

This practice personalizes the resume at the same time it helps avoid clichéd boilerplate language such as that from resume stylebooks. It also employs terminology customary in the client's field, reflecting her familiarity with that field, and among employer representatives likely to interview her.

The resulting resume then usually reflects the client's experience and qualifications much more accurately. More to the point, when the client is being interviewed, what he says and how he says it are more in tune with the language of the resume.

You will be categorizing the information as you follow along the steps laid out in this chapter. Just set aside separate sheets for each category. As you are working on one category, you may come across comments or thoughts that belong with another discussed earlier and can jot it on the proper page.

Let's begin!

# What kind of a job interests you?

This is either the easiest or the hardest question you'll have to answer in the whole process. It is also the most important. Having an answer makes it much easier to craft a resume. So many people have such a very hard time finding an answer to this question. Yet, it is so central to taking charge of your career. Not knowing the answer is likely to put you into a career track that leads nowhere.

Determining what you really want to do is beyond the scope of this book. Where you have in mind two or more definite possibilities, the best advice I can offer is to go through the steps outlined below with each of the possibilities that most interest you in mind, considering each of the questions raised in relation to each career choice.

It may happen that something pops out to you as you move through the process, that you find one career that you resonate to more than the others. If not, you may want to seek out the services of a professional career counselor.

An effective resume is built around the category of career that is being sought. Every part of an effective resume tells the reader why you are the very best qualified candidate for that particular line of work.

This process is similar to what a sales expert does in marketing a product. Before a product can be successfully marketed, it is imperative to come up with its selling points. Not only does the sales specialist need to interest a consumer in the product, she has to tell him why he would want to buy that product instead of other similar products on the market.

Even before that, it is imperative to know what product is being marketed. One can't know the assets of a product without knowing what the product is. You can't sell your services to an employer without knowing what job you're looking for and your qualifications for that job.

It's easy enough and true enough to say the product you are attempting to market is *you!* More than that, the product you are marketing is your ability to perform well in a particular function.

Believe it or not, your fantasies may prove the best key for getting into a line of work that is rewarding for you and moves your career forward. By tapping into your fantasies, you tap into your unconscious mind, the part of you which knows most truly what is good for you. Take the time to fantasize about the job that is ideal for you. What is it like? Is it what you're doing now or something else entirely? What do you see yourself doing five years from now, ten years from now, twenty years from now if everything goes your way and you get your heart's desire?

For many people, the answer may turn out to be what you've been doing for the past several years or some natural offshoot of that. For others, your dream career is radically different. Only you can say for sure.

This precious time of beginning the process of searching for a new job is a great time to look at your career to determine whether you are really going in a career direction that suits you. This is true whether your current job search is on your own initiative or whether it was forced on you.

Choices that were right for you five, ten or twenty years ago may be the source of tremendous dissatisfaction for you today. Now you may know a whole lot more about what is available for you out there than you did back then.

***ONLY YOU*** can keep you tied to a particular career. So many people stay in work they are not suited for or happy with out of inertia coupled with fear that they can't do any better and may do worse.

Even in lean times, there's a wonderful wide world of jobs out there, one of which will bring you satisfaction if you follow your dreams. You don't have to stay in a job that you fight every day, a job that depletes your emotional strength and wears you down, a job that you find less than satisfying.

As you fantasize about possible jobs and a positive new career direction, jot down the key phrases of what that job category's requirements might be. Exactly what is a person who holds down such a position expected to know and to do? You'll be casting your responses to all the remaining questions in light of your response to this one.

What if you can't decide which one of a couple or more very different jobs you'd like to try? Make a separate page or paragraph for each job that interests you.

If you are willing to explore the market for more than one type of job, sound practice is to prepare separate resumes for each one. This gives you the opportunity to highlight those of your qualifications specific to each category of job that interests you on the resume you send to those employers who offer such a position. Prepare separate sets of answers to the questions proposed for each category of job that interests you.

## What was your job experience?

Starting with your most recent job, working backwards through the previous two or three (if that applies), describe just what it is that you do. Keep an eye on just how this experience of yours is relevant to the job you are seeking.

This needn't be a comprehensive review of your work history. Rather, the intent is to demonstrate that you are ready to fill the requirements of the job you are seeking because of the content of past responsibilities. Usually, two or three samplings of your experience are sufficient for this.

First, the vital statistics:

➢ What is or was your position title?

➢ What is the name of your past employer?

> When did you work there (usually month and year to month and year)?

With these three responses, you establish the bare-facts data of your employment history. Now flesh out your information of your responsibilities:

> What are or were your specific duties, responsibilities and accomplishments?

> What exactly do or did you do in a typical day, week or month?

Your response to that last question forms the heart of the experience portion of your resume. In responding, be as specific as you can, keeping in mind the relevance of the responsibilities you are describing to the job or jobs you are seeking.

The following questions can serve as a guide to the kind of information that you need to cover. In order for this list to be comprehensive for a variety of job seekers, some of the questions very probably don't apply to your experience. Answer those that do.

> How many people do or did you supervise? If the number varied, what was the maximum number?

> What activities are or were you responsible for performing and/or overseeing? How would you list them in writing a job description?

> What is or was your production level? How many units did you process per hour, day, week, month or year? What dollar volume of business did you generate or manage?

> What improvements did you make in costs, productivity, production efficiency, and/or operations with what results? What percentage of improvement, number of units, dollar volume and/or cost savings came about from your ideas, work, direction and/or improvements?

> What machinery and/or equipment did you operate?

> What were your specific accomplishments in carrying out your responsibilities? How did you spend a typical day or week?

> What were your special accomplishments? What did you give to this job that was special?

> What recognition or awards did you receive for your job performance?

Examples of how answers to these questions are used may be found in the sample resumes of SECTION C. Be as comprehensive as you can at this stage. Later, you can decide which part of this information you will include in your one-page resume.

## Your education

List the particulars of any schooling you have had. If you attended college, start with your college. If not, start with your high school. List the degree, diploma or certificate you earned, your field of study, the name of the institution and the year you graduated or, if you did not graduate, the years of attendance.

If you did not finish high school and had subsequent specialized training, you can probably safely omit your high school from your resume (and, thereby, not draw attention to the fact that you did not complete that area of education). Under some circumstances, if your college studies were in a different field and so not relevant to the job you're seeking, that institution may also be omitted in deference to special training that you underwent in your actual field.

Usually, the fact that you've completed high school or college does make a favorable impression on employers. It suggests a certain level of sophistication and that you finish what you start.

List any specialized training courses that have provided you with useful skills for the work you are seeking.

The year of your graduation may be listed. In some cases, particularly for older workers, these dates are not stated in a resume. This is discussed more fully in SECTION B.

## Your licenses and certificates

For some jobs, specific licenses or certificates are absolute requirements. If you need a specific license or certificate to qualify for a job, you usually know it.

This is particularly true of those fields related to medicine and education, as well as for operators of heavy equipment and some jobs in the public sector. If the job you seek has such a requirement which you meet, note the name of the license or certificate and the year in which it was granted or the year of its most recent renewal.

## Your job-related hobbies and memberships

Hobbies and organizational memberships are omitted from a resume unless they have some relation to the job being sought.

A professional cites memberships in professional organizations. If your certification came from a professional organization, your membership in that organization is very relevant. An outside sales specialist or a top management candidate usually finds that membership in community organizations brings about community involvement which benefits the new employer by providing contacts in the community. Thus, these are cited.

In unusual cases, hobbies and memberships in hobby associations are relevant if the hobby itself is relevant to the job being sought. Otherwise they are not cited on the resume or brought up during the interview (unless it comes up that your interviewer has an interest in that hobby or is a member of that organization).

Memberships in religious groups or groups which would identify a possible cause for disqualifying you for reasons of discrimination are omitted unless applying for a position within that religion or area.

# *Your know-how*

Go back over all the notes you've made so far to pull out and list every skill listed or suggested in them that may be related to the job you are seeking. What vital skills needed for the job do you have? Obviously, skill requirements vary with the job. What do you know how to do?

Every skill that you list tells the employer that it's not necessary to provide training for that skill. That makes you more attractive in the prospective employer's eyes.

Since every position has its own list of skill requirements, the following list cannot be exhaustive of all possibilities. If you are not familiar with the job because you want to make a job change, take the time to research and think through what skills are applicable to the job you want.

Examples of job-related skills might be:

➢ Management skills: what do you know about interviewing, hiring, motivating, scheduling, assessing performance and (perhaps more important) dismissing employees? What do you know about setting goals, providing direction, implementing goals and reaching objectives?

➢ Maintaining a safe work environment, cutting costs, assuring and improving product quality, increasing productivity?

➢ Sales strategies, purchasing procedures or maintaining inventory. Have you a list of outside contacts that will be useful in the position?

➢ Skills in dealing with people including negotiating and problem resolution?

➢ Communication skills: Organizing and presenting ideas coherently and logically?

➢ Preparing reports and proposals? Editing?

➢ Equipment operation? If the operation of specific equipment is complex, what aspects of that operation are you familiar with?

An example of this last skill set might be familiarity with computer operations. What computer types or systems are you competent in performing? Do you know how to enter data, operate specific programs or all programs, write programs, diagnose and fix problems or any combination of these operations?

Identification of your skill set is one of the distinguishing advantages of the **HIGH-IMPACT Resume** that makes your resume stand out among those being assessed by a resume reviewer.

## What are your best qualities?

What personal qualities make you most valuable to an employer? Don't be bashful in listing them. Jot down every good quality that you can think of and ask your friends for a few. Just make sure that these qualities truly describe you and that you can live up to them.

This may well be the most important segment of your job search. Knowing your best qualities gives you a prime tool for marketing yourself and your services. As selling points, your personal qualities are extremely important in distinguishing you from your competition for any job.

The **HIGH-IMPACT Resume**, laid out fully in the next chapter, owes much of its uniqueness and effectiveness to taking advantage of your unique personal qualities and highlighting them as your chief selling points. This unique feature of the format makes your resume stand out strikingly from other resumes crossing your prospective employer's desk.

Your best qualities may roughly be divided into three categories:

★ Personal qualities,

★ Motivational qualities, and

★ Areas in which you are knowledgeable.

To put it another way, what kind of a person are you? What motivates you? What do you know how to do?

# PUTTING IT TOGETHER: INTRODUCING THE *HIGH-IMPACT RESUME*

By now you have pages of information. Just how do you put it together into an effective resume? In this chapter, we'll look at many principles, techniques and subtle tricks of the trade which have proved to be effective for my clients.

There are no hard and fast rules for writing resumes. Rather, there is room for many approaches. A variety of resume formats cross a prospective employer's desk in any given week. The range of possibilities is limited only by the imagination of those who produce them. The challenge is to produce a resume which stands out strikingly enough from the rest to catch the reviewer's eye.

There are people who are hired in spite of their resumes rather than because of them, just as some products are purchased in the face of a salesperson's poor presentation simply because the buyer is in the market. Some people are standouts even with shabby presentation. Then, too, not every employer is savvy about effective hiring practices.

Even with savvy employers, a well-thought-out, well-constructed and unique resume presentation draws attention precisely because it is different from the rest. So many job applicants use a boilerplate out-of-the-can approach that originality stands out.

Its eye-catching quality helps make a resume effective! Persuading an employer to pick up and read a resume is one distinguishing mark of an effective resume. An innovative resume may very well lead to a paying position. Savvy employers value innovative thinking.

Make sure that the graphics of the finished resume, that is the appearance of the typing and layout, is pleasing to the eye. Obviously, the resume should be neatly typed. There should be no typing errors or misspelled words.

In all the resumes that I've prepared, I've used the same basic graphics with minor variations to suit the client. This style is laid out in the descriptions below and, with some variations to fit the varying requirements for different clients, appears in all the examples in this book. This is a matter of personal taste, not a requirement for all resumes, not even for all **HIGH-IMPACT Resumes**.

However, many other graphic styles are in use. Adapting graphics to your own personal tastes is certainly permissible and may serve you well. As long as the information is clearly presented and the finished product is attractive, readable and presentable, that choice is up to you.

The product of a typewriter, word processor or computer is acceptable. Employers know that not all applicants are knowledgeable about computers or even have access to one. Another option, especially valuable for those who don't type and those desiring a truly polished look, is professional typesetting. Virtually every retail printer offers this service.

In using a computer or word processor, too many variations in style of type can lend a cluttered, disorganized look. Be conservative.

## What information goes into a resume?

What does a prospective employer need to know about you from a resume? First, that the document in front of him is, in fact, a resume. Then, he has to know *your name* and *how to reach you*. Usually, this information is at the top of the page in any resume. Third, he needs to know *what kind of work you are seeking* in order to determine whether your aspirations have any relevance to the job he wants to fill.

Fourth, he needs to know whether you are qualified to do the job he's seeking to have filled. For that, he has to know something about *your experience* and *education*. So there is usually some sort of information about these in a resume.

The foregoing items are the bare bones of any resume. Anything else is filler. Beyond those bare bones, as **TAKE CHARGE Career Manager**, what do *YOU* want to be in your resume?

You want to give your prospective employer information which will make him pull *YOUR* resume out of a stack of resumes and salivate to talk to you! You want to tell him what is so special about you, what is so outstanding that it makes you so much more desirable for his operations than all those other folks out there clamoring to talk to him about that same job!

You want to give him all that information in *just one page* while making optimum use of every inch of that page. Every item on that page should work for you! Now, there's a daunting assignment.

To make that happen, all you have to do is sift through and organize the information you collected in the preceding chapter. This will enable you to determine just what in your background will convince the employer of your dreams that it is in his interest to talk to *YOU!*

## The STANDARD resume formats

To compete successfully in any market, you need to know what the competition is doing. As this is being written, virtually all resumes coming into the hands of prospective employers use one or the other of two standard styles, which are two variations of the **STANDARD** format. The only significant difference between the two is the order of listing previous jobs held.

The most commonly used *Chronological Resume* lists and describes previous jobs in reverse chronological order with the last-held job listed and described first, followed by the job before that and so on.

The ***Functional Resume*** groups jobs with similar responsibilities together without reference to chronology. This style is particularly useful for those who have held jobs with unlike responsibilities in two or more fields and those who seek to cover some flaw in their work history.

These two are the styles advocated and described in books on resumes you pull off the shelf of your library or bookstore. They are also the models for computer-generated resumes.

The **HIGH-IMPACT *Resume*** draws from both styles as appropriate based on the particular needs of the job seeker, this allows for flexibility to serve a variety of backgrounds, qualifications and the career goals of the job seeker. It also includes innovations not found in these traditional styles.

We'll look at the standard resume in both its Chronological and Functional formats briefly before considering in depth the more effective **HIGH-IMPACT *Resume*** developed by this author and used by clients with outstanding results.

The main entries found in virtually every resume following either of the the standard format styles are:

- The **identifying header**: Simply consists of the word, **RESUME**, together with the applicant's name, address, phone number and e-mail address.

- ***Purpose*** or ***Objective***: Roughly, why the applicant is applying for this job and what she hopes to realize from experience gained on the job. Sometimes this includes long-range career goals.

- ***Experience***: This job history can be presented in either chronological or functional form.

- ***Education***.

These four items are the bare bones of the ***Standard Resume***. Depending on the background of the applicant and the nature of the job sought, additional entries may be added. Among them:

- ***Licenses*** and/or ***Certifications***.

- ***Memberships***

- ***Skills***

# *Introducing the HIGH-IMPACT Resume*

While the **HIGH-IMPACT Resume** began with and so has many features in common with the Standard Resume, there are very significant differences. These differences lead you to spell out and highlight the precise information that a prospective employer is looking for in order to lay groundwork for making a positive hiring decision in your favor. The **HIGH-IMPACT Resume** utilizes every entry to maximum advantage in order to put that information up front where he can't miss it.

The **HIGH-IMPACT Resume** differs from the standard formats in that it places far more emphasis on your assets, attitudes and skills, while not losing the attention to your experience and education of the standard resume.

Every employer knows that your attitudes and skills have a high correlation with job performance. This is the information an employer conducts an interview to find out. What's said about experience and education serves to back up what is said about your assets, attitudes and skills. Thus, when a prospective employer picks up your **HIGH-IMPACT Resume**, his eye is drawn immediately to your principal selling points.

Information presented in your **HIGH-IMPACT Resume** serves yet another purpose in your job search. It starts you thinking about how best to promote yourself in interviews and gives you positive talking points to discuss with prospective employers.

The **HIGH-IMPACT** format is made up of two divisions: introductory material and the body. The introductory upper portion consists of the **Heading** and the innovative **Situation Wanted Ad** for you. The body of the resume in the lower portion is made up of an individualized presentation of your qualifications, education and experience.

Let's dissect the **HIGH-IMPACT** format item by item considering its major entries, section by section, and how to tailor them to showcase your particular assets.

## Heading

In the **HIGH-IMPACT** format, the **Heading** consists of two lines as it this example:

---

**RESUME OF JANE Q. VERYSPECIAL**

000 Any Street    Your town, OH 44000    (419) 555-9999   myaddress@fiction.com

---

The first line is capitalized throughout to emphasize you as someone to be reckoned with. Using a typewriter, words are spread out using a space between each two letters and three spaces between words and underlined to highlight the words. With a computer, a simple boldface provides sufficient highlighting.

The second line is in smaller type and, as shown, all in a single line.

## *HIGH-IMPACT TIP*

Reducing the heading to two lines across the top of the page conserves valuable space on our one-page format for your selling points, while providing needed information.

Typical resumes, such as computer-generated resumes, list this information in box form, as on an envelope and take as many as five lines for it, followed by a few more lines of white space, thus reducing the space for other important entries.

When using a computer, make the first line large enough that your name stands out, but don't waste space with overly large type.

Following the heading material, there should be two or three lines of white space, that is with no typing, simply to enhance the graphics.

## *The Situation Wanted Ad for YOU*

The next section of your **HIGH-IMPACT Resume**, a **Situation Wanted Ad** for your skills and best qualities spells out just what personal and professional assets you offer. Information for this segment is drawn primarily from three sections of your notes: the description of the job you are seeking, your best personal qualities and what you know how to do.

The **Situation Wanted Ad** is the unique distinguishing characteristic of the **HIGH-IMPACT** approach. From reports from my clients, this seems to be the key feature that makes this approach so successful.

It does this by making the most of the opportunity you have in just this one-page format to put your key information in front of the employer–information about your attitudes and work philosophy, as well as your best qualities.

How does the **Situation Wanted Ad** differ from the standard resume format? Step back a moment and look at the standard resume. The nearest equivalent in the standard format is the entry headed as **Purpose** or **Objectives**.

In attempting to fashion a standard resume, most people approach this section with more than a little bewilderment. "What am I supposed to say here?" "What are they expecting to see?" "What will make the best impression on the employer?" "What must I avoid in order not to make a bad impression?"

After mulling it over, most job seekers conclude the entry has something to do with their goals. In fact, some guidebooks say just that. The major goal of a whole lot of people preparing a resume is simply to get a job and succeed in it. That goal can be stated in various ways.

In the words of an actual resume from my files, it usually comes out as something like:

> **Purpose:** Seeking a challenging and responsible position where education and experience can be immediately and profitably utilized.

This gobbledygook is as unsatisfactory from an employer's point of view as it is from the applicant's. It tells an employer nothing useful about whether this is a good candidate for the job he has in mind. Indeed, it lays an implicit burden on him!

What does an employer have to do to make a position "challenging and responsible" for this applicant? What happens if he fails? Will he end up with an unhappy, unproductive employee?

Particularly unsatisfactory is that such a statement gives no information about why this applicant is to be preferred over other applicants. At best, ***Purpose*** states the kind of job being sought. Only too often, as in the example above, the entry is so ambiguous, it doesn't even do that!

Accordingly, most resume reviewers simply ignore such a statement, paying it no heed and giving it absolutely no weight. *That makes **Purpose** so much wasted space in your one-page format!*

The second problem with ***Purpose*** is that it is basically an "I approach," long proven a very ineffective technique in getting what you want. That is, it tells what you *expect to gain* from employment, rather than what you *have to offer* that employer.

Worse still, this entry puts a none-too-subtle demand on an employer by implying that he, rather than you, is responsible for seeing to it that your needs and desires for satisfying work and advancement are met. In effect, you put him in charge of your career. No one besides you wants or needs that responsibility.

In sum, the bottom line boils down to this: ***Purpose** serves no useful purpose at all in a resume!*

Compare the text of ***Purpose*** above with the text of the **Situation Wanted Ad**, following, taken from the **HIGH-IMPACT Resume** prepared for the same applicant. Given that the remaining information in the two resumes is similar, if you were an employer reading from these two resumes (one with the stated ***Purpose*** and the other with the **Situation Wanted Ad** below), which candidate would you want to talk to?

> Versatile, dynamic, creative, knowledgeable and hardworking experienced **Professional Business Manager**, a cost-conscious results-getter who knows how to streamline procedures for optimal efficiency and effectiveness, a gifted trainer and motivator who knows how to inspire staff to peak performance, a problem-solver who works through people to find viable solutions that staff will implement and a leader of thorough integrity who cares about people, deals with them fairly and with humor and establishes good working relationships seeks to put his strengths to work for a quality forward-moving firm.

Note how much useful information not found in the standard format is given here. Employers tend to react favorably to such information. They set up interviews to have an opportunity to check it out for themselves. When they do, they're already thinking in positive terms about you and your qualifications for a job they have in mind for you.

Information given in the ***Situation Wanted Ad*** also serves as a basis for positive talking points during the interview, putting you and your qualifications in the best light. The ***Situation Wanted Ad*** format allows extensive flexibility to adapt it to individual needs and preferences. The following outline of its contents is intended as a guide rather than a rigid prescription.

Dissecting the ***Situation Wanted Ad***, we see it has four basic elements: a string of introductory descriptive adjectives, a highlighted designation of the position sought, a string of noun descriptor phrases and a request for the job.

The first line consists of four or five adjectives spelling out the best qualities of the applicant and designed to catch the attention of the resume reviewer. Use as many as will fit in that first line. They should be positive qualities any employee would desire in an employee. They are taken from the list of your best qualities that you drew up in assessing your qualifications.

### *HIGH-IMPACT TIP*

Throughout the ***Situation Wanted Ad***, use descriptors that truly reflect your personality, not just high-sounding qualities you think sound good but that you will have difficulty living up to. Your employer will expect you to deliver what you have promised. Presenting yourself as something that you are not will start you off on the wrong foot and could end in disaster for you.

As an example, some folks are born dynamic go-getters. They hit the ground running and have an almost compulsive need to achieve. They thrive on pressure and are naturals for certain high-pressure jobs. If this describes you, the word "*dynamic*" is your leadoff adjective.

That word, "*dynamic*," sounds good. You may be tempted to use it even though it doesn't really describe you. If your actual personality style is laid back, you could find yourself competing for and, worse, getting into a job you don't really want. There, you'd be doing work in which you have little interest in competition with high-powered people who thrive on its challenges. That leads to maximum job stress, even to illness, while making it very difficult for you to get productive or satisfying results.

Keep in mind that there are many satisfying, high-paying jobs for folks who do not thrive on pressure. If you are such a person, go after one of them and use descriptors that lead to those jobs.

The second line consists of two elements: the word *"experienced"* (when it applies) and the highlighted name of the position you are seeking. Use capital letters to highlight on a typewriter.

Highlighting the name of the position sought enables an employer to see at a glance where you might fit into his plans, whether you match a position he wishes to fill or should be referred to the correct department for that line of work. A distinct advantage for you is that, if sufficiently impressed by your resume and at the time, doesn't have an appropriate position for you, he may pass it on to another employer. This was the experience of at least one of my clients.

> ### *HIGH-IMPACT TIP*
>
> The word "Specialist" as in "Sales Specialist" rather than "Salesman" is often useful as a part of a position name. Where appropriate, it adds a certain tone to the resume by implying a deeper knowledge of the field.

The third element of the **Situation Wanted Ad** is made up of (usually) three descriptor phrases, following the format:

**"A (descriptor noun) who ..., a (descriptor) who..., and a (descriptor) who..."**

This formula is very flexible and can be varied to meet the situation. In the example above, there are four such descriptor phrases. This would be a maximum. Three such phrases are preferable to four.

Descriptor phrases should be short and crisp. To word them, refer to the interview notes you took about your best qualities, blending in those skills most pertinent to high job performance.

The fourth component of the **Situation Wanted Ad** is called ***the ask*** in sales parlance. Just as it is important in sales to ask for the sale, here it is important to ask for the job! Use a phrase similar to "seeks to put her skills to work for a forward-moving quality firm." In it, you are effectively asking for the job. The phrase strongly suggests that you are a quality achiever looking for a quality position and also expectations of quality from your employer. It also subtly suggests that you are a discriminating job seeker who won't settle for substandard working conditions.

The **Situation Wanted Ad** is followed by an understated horizontal line stretching from left to right margin across the page. This serves three purposes: First, it enhances the graphics by breaking up the page visually so that it is more pleasing to the eye. Second, it divides the introductory upper section from the more detailed body of the resume containing specifics of your background and qualifications. Third, it draws attention both to the **Situation Wanted Ad** above it and the item immediately below.

To make this line, simply make use of the symbols or special characters available on the machine you are using. You may find it amusing to experiment. Keep it understated and unobtrusive.

## *The body of the Resume*

The body of the resume provides specifics of your experience and qualifications. As in one version of the standard format, it consists of two columns, one narrow and one wide. The narrow column contains the headings of the various sectors: ***Experience:, Education:,*** and the like.

This is merely a personal style preference. Other styles will work equally well. In this regard, content is more important than style.

The usual order of entries to this section is:

➢ Hands-On Knowledge of:

➢ Experience:

➢ Education:

Particular entries such as:

➢ Other Experience: used mainly for filler, omitted if there is enough direct experience.

➢ Memberships:

➢ Licenses:

➢ Certificates:

Demonstrating the flexibility of the ***HIGH-IMPACT*** format, in special situations entry order can be varied. As noted above, the horizontal line following the ***Situation Wanted Ad*** draws the eye to the item immediately below it. That's where to put qualifications of most interest to the employer.

For example, for someone entering the job field with little experience, ***Education:*** is the qualification most likely to lead to a paying position. Thus, it goes immediately below the horizontal line. For a teacher or nurse, the proper license or certificate is required by law. That goes just below the horizontal line.

The challenge of ***HIGH-IMPACT Resume*** writing is to turn personality characteristics, background and skills, whatever they may be, into assets. It is to pull out of your personality, skills and background whatever assets there may be that translate into job performance and contributions to your employer's success.

Meeting that challenge enables you to compete successfully for those jobs that interest you and advance your career. Usually, you're not in competition with your diametric opposite. That person is likely not going for the job that interests you. Your competitors are apt to have personalities and interests similar to yours.

The best course in resume writing is to make your resume reflect your personality and background as accurately as you can. So doing will help you determine whether the job you thought you might like is really right for you.

## Hands-On Knowledge

In the standard resume, these entries are labeled *Skills*. The term, *Hands-on Knowledge of:* is a shade more trendy suggesting a deeper level of knowledge and skill. You know how to do these things not just in theory, but actually have hands-on experience with them. Because the term is still a bit more unusual in resumes, it is more likely to draw attention from a resume reviewer.

*Hands on Knowledge of:* is a list of those skills with relevance to the job you're seeking and to the business world in general. Any skill suggesting that you are versatile, flexible and capable of handling a broader range of responsibilities than is spelled out in the job description is usually a plus for you.

Up to a point, versatility makes you more valuable to employers. Versatility suggests a good candidate for advancement. If you're interested in advanced positions, it's helpful to plant the seed in your resume.

Be wary of overdoing it! Too much variety in listing your skills suggests that you are unfocused and lack a sense of personal direction. That suggests further that you're easily bored and require constant stimulation on the job.

Make the most of whatever assets you have! Look for a job requiring highly focused skills. There are jobs for experts in virtually any field.

To conserve space for other information, group similar skills into a single entry. For example, a purchasing agent needs skills in identifying purchasing needs, when they are needed, identifying suppliers and negotiating for the best deal. All of this can be said in one line. On the other hand, if filler is needed to make your resume appear to contain more information than it actually does, such skills can be listed individually and elaborated upon.

## Your experience

This is the key part of your resume, the one part that a resume reviewer is likely to read if she doesn't read anything else.

### *HIGH-IMPACT TIP*

For the label for this section, instead of simply using the term, ***Experience:***, modify that term with a word indicating the kind of experience you have that is related to the job you're seeking. Examples are ***Management Experience:, Civil Engineering Experience:*** or ***Public Health Nursing Experience:***.

This has the effect of reinforcing your ***Situation Wanted Ad*** by suggesting that your experience is relevant to the position you are seeking.

### *HIGH-IMPACT TIP*

If you also have significant experience unrelated to the position you are seeking, put a label on this. It could simply read ***Other Experience:***.

If this experience, while not directly related to the position you are seeking, nevertheless has given you useful skills which broaden your approach to that position, use an experience-labeling modifier. For example, ***Business Experience:*** could prove very useful for someone going into teaching high school students because it provides a perspective that other teachers would not necessarily have.

Another example is ***Military Service:*** for those who have spent time in one of the service branches. Whatever their experience, time spent in the military usually sharpens leadership skills.

---

The first line of the entry describing your experience usually identifies the position you held (or hold), the establishment you worked for, the town where it is located and the dates of your employment. Dates of employment are expressed as month-and-year to month-and-year because this is the employers' preference. For example:

| | |
|---|---|
| PRODUCTION EXPERIENCE: | Production worker, XYZ Corporation, Anytown, Anystate. June 2015 to July 2022: |

The name of your employer is in italics, bold faced or underlined, depending on the style you use to prepare your resume. If you're still employed, the dates of employment might read: June 2015 to present.

Preferably all words, including state names, are spelled out in full as space allows. The two last items may be omitted under special circumstances. For example, if you live in Anytown, you're looking for a job there and all your work experience has been with Anytown employers, the town can be omitted. In like fashion, if all your work experience has been in the state where you are seeking employment, the state can be omitted.

There are also instances where it is advisable to omit dates of employment. Two very common examples are when there are large gaps between periods of employment and when dates of employment suggest that you are nearing or over forty years of age (discussed more fully in SECTION B).

To prepare the text of the description of your work experience, draw on the notes you made in assessing your qualifications. The more complete these notes, the more information you can draw on.

The purpose of the description of your past experience is to show that you are a dedicated, self-motivated results producer who will be an asset to your new employer within the scope of the job you're seeking. Proactive employees with an eye for what needs to be done and the initiative to follow through on that are assets to any employer.

A caveat, while on the job, before taking on any project outside your job description, it's good to check it out with your employer and get her permission first. She may want to verify that it will not unduly take away from the duties you were hired to perform or her other plans to deal with the problem.

Use short, concise sentences and paragraphs emphasizing your activities and level of responsibility. The pronoun "I" is understood. Sentences begin with a verb. Use action verbs as much as possible. As an example, the following is from the resume of a general manager of a large equipment dealership.

| | |
|---|---|
| MANAGEMENT EXPERIENCE: | Directed the activities of up to 18 employees in all aspects of the operations of a large equipment dealership.<br>Responsible for sales, service and part supply functions.<br>Realized $7,000,000 annually in equipment sales, $3,000,000 in parts sales and $2,750,000 in service fees.<br>Interviewed, hired, evaluated, motivated, scheduled and dismissed employees.<br>Oversaw computation of payroll hours for entry into computer.<br>Scheduled service and sales functions, including meeting and promotional functions.<br>Demonstrated equipment for buyers.<br>Oversaw accounts payable and receivable. Computed agency taxes.<br>Operated accounting programs to settle sales of large equipment.<br>Negotiated with and purchased supplies from vendors. |

Note the action verbs in the above resume: *Oversaw, Responsible for, Realized, Interviewed, hired, evaluated, motivated and dismissed. Scheduled, Demonstrated, Computed, Negotiated*. All of these suggest that this is a very proactive person who takes responsibility for his productivity without waiting to be told what he should be doing. Such a person is an asset to any business.

Note too, the numbers in the first paragraph. These state that this is a person who directed eighteen employees and was responsible for more than thirteen million dollars in sales. *Impressive!* Although he identified himself as a "Sales Specialist/Sales Manager" candidate in his **Situation Wanted Ad**, this person is a candidate for the next higher level position in management with responsibility for more employees and even larger dollar amounts, such as vice-president for sales.

---

### *HIGH-IMPACT TIP*

Quantifying your productivity (18 employees, $7,000,000 in sales, savings of more than 25%) makes a very positive impression on employers who immediately think of the impact you'll have on their bottom line and the level of responsibility you can carry.

In stating quantities, use numerals rather than spelling numbers out (*18* rather than *eighteen*). This makes for visual impact, drawing attention to these numbers at even a casual glance.

A resume should cover your most important responsibilities, not necessarily every single task you performed. The more responsibilities listed, the less description required for each task, as in the example above. With fewer responsibilities, the more detailed the description needs to be to add substance.

---

Following is an example of a more narrowly focused job, that of a production worker (another name for an assembly line worker). Virtually everything she does is spelled out.

---

Operate color mixer to prepare plastic pellets for automotive applications.
Obtain resin and color from pre-batch operator. Verify to specs.
Operate tow motor to transport to mixer. Load and operate mixer.
Inspect output. Operate grinder to regrind rejects.
Assist with inventory as needed.
Train new employees to job.

Spelling out the details of her activities suggests that she is a dedicated worker at this level who knows her job and, once instructed on what to do and how to do it, performs all assigned tasks faithfully. That's a vital asset in a production worker who is not expected to be proactive, but to take direction.

Nonetheless, any indication of initiative, such as making suggestions that realized cost savings or improved product reliability or safety procedures, suggests dedication to the job and the employer and is usually a plus.

Equipment operation as part of the job should also be spelled out. Illustrating both of these items is an experience description taken from the resume of a maintenance mechanic.

> Repaired and maintained heavy stone loading and crushing equipment.
>
> Performed routine scheduled preventative maintenance. Diagnosed malfunctions and made necessary repairs where possible. Utilized welder, presser, lathes and other mechanical tools as needed.
>
> On own initiative, instituted inventory system, organizing and systematizing parts inventory, thereby realizing savings in worker time for retrieving needed parts.
>
> Analyzed inventory, categorized parts by part numbers, had shelving constructed and organized parts on shelves.

Note that after stating that he instituted an inventory system on his own initiative, the next sentence states the activities he followed in order to accomplish that. This is a valuable employee. His initiative saved costs for the company by making it easier for him and coworkers to perform. Outstanding achievements associated with your duties with extensive ramifications for efficiency, cost savings and the like are spelled out. An example from the resume of a plant manager:

> Consolidated three companies in three locations into one by overseeing the transfer of equipment and personnel.
>
> Reduced manufacturing costs by 30% by reducing manufacturing time per unit from 3 to 2.1 hours over a period of five years. Oversaw implementation of more efficient materials handling procedures.
>
> Consolidated operations. Installed improved equipment to achieve this objective.
>
> Headed safety committee to reduce workman's compensation claims from a 65% penalty to a 17% credit over a period of five years through better equipment, implementing safety policies and installing safety training for foremen.

As illustrated in these four examples and all of the resumes in SECTION C, with the description of your duties on your current and previous jobs, you are, in effect, explicitly telling prospective employers:

- The level of responsibility you demonstrated.

- That you apply your know-how in practice, that is, that you truly are capable of performing in that kind of job.

You want your resume to say implicitly that:

- You are responsible and productive and can be trusted.

- You are proactive, have initiative and are willing to act.

- You keep the best interests of employer, coworkers and clients in view.

- Your job-related expectations are realistic and reasonable.

- You plan to be an asset to the employer and perform up to job requirements, if not beyond.

With that information, you're singing the employer's song. If he's convinced, you will certainly be offered a position, sometimes even if one has to be created for you.

All you need in a resume is enough information to convey such implicit messages. Anything beyond is excess. With a **_HIGH-IMPACT Resume_**, that job can readily be done in a single page. It also has been done by millions of resumes in a variety of styles.

### *HIGH-IMPACT TIP*

It is both unnecessary and unproductive to describe every job you've ever held, whether with just one company or with several. One, two or occasionally three of the most recent and relevant are sufficient. More can decidedly work against you by suggesting either that you cannot hold a job or that you're ready to be retired.

You can make creative use of white space (a printer's term for that part of the page which is not used by type). With less data white space can be used between lines and between sections in order to spread the text through the page. With more data, you may have to tighten the text, leaving out less crucial information.

## Your Education

This section of your resume generally consists of a simple line by line listing of the schooling and training you've had which is pertinent to the job being sought.

If you have college training or a degree, you would start with that, listing the degree, if any, the course of study, the institution (emphasized by italics, boldface or underlining), and the year of your graduation or years of attendance if you did not graduate. High school is omitted on the presumption that you previously earned a high school diploma or convinced the college that you had sufficient learning not to need one.

In the example, the first line states that a degree was earned; the second implies that your studies did not result in a degree:

| | |
|---|---|
| EDUCATION: | B.Sc., education, Anystate University, 2015 |
| | Business administration, University of Yourstate, 2016-8 |

If you have not been to college, start with your high school. You can add the curriculum if that is significant, as in the example of a machinist/supervisor:

| | |
|---|---|
| EDUCATION: | Machine trades curriculum, Vocational High School, 2007 |
| | Machinist certification, State Apprentice Council |
| | Basic electricity and electronics, U.S. Marine Corps |

If you are not a high school graduate, other training can be listed:

| | |
|---|---|
| EDUCATION: | Heating and air conditioning trade school |
| | Various safety training courses. |

In those rare cases where sufficient other information is included in the resume, this entry can be omitted altogether. Since omission is sure to be questioned, the entry should be omitted only when inclusion raises more questions for the employer than omission.

## Other possible entries

There are a number of other possible entries which can be included in a resume to reflect special qualifications of the applicant or requirements of the job sought or simply to fill in a scanty resume. Some examples of heading in the left margin are:

➤ LICENSES: such as the chauffeur's license required for truck driving.

- ➢ CERTIFICATES: such as a certificate qualifying you to teach a particular level.

- ➢ ACCOMPLISHMENTS: such as truly outstanding achievements with more extensive ramifications that can be stated in the experience section. Examples are significant honors and leadership on a community board which, mainly through your efforts, introduced significant new services or improvements.

- ➢ HOBBIES: These should be mentioned when they are relevant to the job and there is not sufficient job-related experience.

## *Omit these entries*

There are two sets of entries popular with many that take up valuable space that is both better used to make your case for employment and may actually work against you:

- ➢ VITAL STATISTICS: Your sex, race, marital status and the like. Employers are not permitted by law to ask you about them. Such gratuitous information may give certain biased employers an opportunity to discriminate against you while reviewing your resume, the safest time for them to do so without penalty.

- ➢ REFERENCES: Also omit phrases such as "References available on request."

No matter what your resume says, if an employer asks for references, are you going to turn him down? Employers implicitly expect you to provide references and routinely ask for them on their application forms. Saying that you have them provides useless information.

Yes, you must be prepared to name three personal references to vouch for your character and three business references to vouch for the quality of your work. Virtually all employers require personal references. Some ask for business references as well. These names go on the application form you fill out before your interview, not on your resume.

Copies of letters of recommendation and citations for outstanding performance may accompany your resume and cover letter when you send these to prospective employers. Keep the total of such documents to three or less. That's enough to make the point without burdening the employer with reading material.

Be absolutely certain that such letters will truly benefit you. Read them over carefully before sending them in order to make sure that they include no statements which will cause your resume to be rejected.

## *Final touches*

At this point, you've drawn up a resume master copy in its final form: typed, proofread and ready for the printer. What's next?

The final step is to take it to the printer and have sufficient copies made to be sent out to employers.

At this point, not only is your resume printed and ready for mailing, but in the process of drawing it up, you have gained a good idea of what you have to offer an employer. You are ready for the next step in your job search discussed in SECTION D.

---

### *HIGH-IMPACT TIP*

Choose a quality light-colored business stationery for your resume. It doesn't matter if it is gray, beige, blue or some other non-garish shade. Any business color of your choice is satisfactory. Any printer has a selection of various colors in stock with envelopes to match. Be sure to purchase enough matching envelopes!

You may also want to purchase matching or contrasting stationery at the time for your cover letters.

High quality colored stationery will make your resume stand out among all the others, most of which come through on white copier paper. That alone may well lead a resume reviewer to pull your resume out of his stack and examine its contents.

The use of stationery makes a subtle point that you are a class act. Anything that makes your resume stand out positively from the rest is a plus in your favor.

---

### *HIGH-IMPACT TIP*

Use commemorative stamps on everything you mail to employers. Once again, this draws positive attention to your resume because a lot of people collect such stamps. This will lead them to pick up your resume for the stamp.

# WHAT ABOUT A COVER LETTER?

"Do I really need a cover letter?" That's a common question asked by at least half of the job searchers I have encountered.

The obvious answer is, "No, you don't absolutely need one!" Employers receive many thousands of resumes without accompanying cover letters every day. As noted often in these pages, people get jobs by all sorts of means. Millions of people have gotten jobs without using cover letters.

"So," you ask, "do I really *want* to send a cover letter with my resume and why? What advantage is there to taking the time and effort to put one together?"

**YES! You definitely do!** A well-crafted cover letter does a lot for you! Most important, it reinforces your qualifications for the position by laying them out specifically for the employer.

Sales experts speak of searching out or creating an *edge*. Your edge is the tiniest advantage you offer over your competition that persuades the buyer to select your product or services over theirs. The purpose of your cover letter is to give you that edge with the employer. Just the fact that you have included a cover letter when your competition has not is bound to make a positive impression for you. It strongly suggests that you are a person with class who goes the extra mile.

Suppose you decide that a cover letter is unnecessary and simply send your resume! You run the risk of seeing the job go to the applicant who did take the time and trouble to come up with a case for himself by creating an edge with a cover letter.

A cover letter is ***a second opportunity to present your case for being hired!*** Stated another way, a cover letter is a second opportunity to present your services to an employer. It's a second opportunity to make a case for your services, highlighting and reinforcing why *YOU* are the most qualified job applicant to apply. It's a second opportunity to spell out specifics of your background and know-how that make the best choice to assist this particular business enterprise in turning a profit. A cover letter places a second sheet of paper spelling out and emphasizing your most important selling points directly into the hands of the people who will hire you.

Even more important, a cover letter provides an opportunity to request an interview directly from the very person you most want to talk to, the one who does the interviewing and hiring. Although, in a sense, simply sending a resume is a request for an interview, employers are more likely to respond to a request made directly to them.

There is *EVERYTHING* to be gained by taking the time to prepare a solid well-thought-out cover letter. A well-prepared letter can definitely make the difference between your being hired and the job you want going to another applicant.

The task of preparing a cover letter continues to prepare you for eventual employment interviews by helping you do your homework on just what you have to offer employers.

Since a cover letter is directed to a particular employer, it is considerably more effective to write an individual letter tailored to each employer you are considering than to use a mass-produced form letter similar to your resume. The fact that you've taken time to consider that employer's individual business requirements and have personalized your letter to these requirements certainly enhances your case with that employer and makes it more likely that she will want to talk to you. If she doesn't currently have a suitable open position, she may be impressed enough to keep you in mind for the future or even pass your resume and cover letter on to another employer.

(Note: when working through an employment agency, that organization essentially performs the same functions as a cover letter making it unnecessary for you to prepare one.)

What goes into a well-thought-out cover letter? Unlike for resumes, there is no standard format other than the standard business letter format. Using that format and effective presentation principles for public speaking as models, this author developed a pattern for the body of the letter in order to optimize results for my clients. This **HIGH-IMPACT Cover Letter** format is described in the following pages.

The standard business letter format consists of a letterhead with name, address and contact information, the date, the body of the letter, the closing and signature, plus an indication of enclosures, if any (in this case, your resume and any letters of recommendation). There are a number of standard texts on this format which you can check out at your local library, or you can find models on the Internet.

# The HIGH-IMPACT Cover Letter

The ***HIGH-IMPACT Cover Letter*** takes just one page. Employers generally are much more impressed by your ability to organize your selling points into just one page than they are with a long chatty letter that takes up valuable time through attempting to cover every possible point exhaustively. Brevity is also the soul of effectiveness.

The ***HIGH-IMPACT Cover Letter*** begins with a letterhead in order to give the letter an appearance of professionalism. Such a letterhead can easily be created. You may use the common style of entering it at the top of the page or you may want to explore other options in order to develop the letterhead style that suits you. Anything that looks professional will serve.

For example:

---

Joseph M. Jobseeker
444 Any Street. Anytown, NY 00000
(555) 555-5555
myemailaddress@fiction.net

---

A letterhead may also be typeset for you by any printer.

The letterhead is followed by the date, usually on the right side of the page. A salutation, such as "Dear Sir" is optional.

### HIGH-IMPACT TIP

Whenever possible, direct the letter to the person who does the actual hiring. Use her name and title (such as *Grace Q. Bigboss, Manager, Sales Department*) in the address block and in the salutation (such as *Dear Ms. Bigboss*).

When you can't determine who will do the hiring, as in answering a blind newspaper ad, leave off the salutation. You just might be addressing a *Madame* rather than a *Sir*. If you are specifically directed to send your resume to a particular person (often someone in the personnel department) it's usually a good idea to do so even if he is not the person to make the hiring decision. Many firms insist on screening by the personnel department before an interview possibility is considered.

> **HIGH-IMPACT TIP**
>
> You can often find the name of the person who will do the hiring by doing a little research. Telephone the company and ask the person who answers the phone for the name and title of the department you are interested in. You can also check this out at your local library or on the Internet. Caution: Be aware that such lists can be outdated by staff turnover.

Any research at all you do on the employer and her probable requirements even before sitting down to compose a cover letter, research which is reflected in that letter, tells an employer a few good things about you and sets you apart from other applicants.

First, it says for you that you care enough and are interested enough to want to know something about her enterprise. Second, it tells her that you're organized enough and took the initiative to carry through to find out the information. The two factors could be enough to persuade her that you are a conscientious potential employee that she just may want to talk to.

Since the simple step of doing such research does not occur to the vast majority of applicants who simply send out tons of resumes in all directions, that might induce a prospective employer to want to look at your resume.

Having data about the employer beforehand also prepares you to conduct your side of the interview more effectively. It prepares you to cover more items of interest to both you and the employer. It enables you to pinpoint and discuss those aspects of her needs for which you are prepared to provide assistance and solutions. The resulting interview may even lead to her entrusting you with more responsibilities and a higher paying job.

## The body of the letter

The secret of writing an effective cover letter is in adopting a "you approach." So, speak in terms of the employer's needs rather than your own.

The primary objective of a cover letter is to convince a prospective employer that you understand her dilemma and have the capability and motivation to help her find solutions for it. The employer's dilemma is that, in order to have a successful business, she needs to find a capable and motivated someone to fulfill a particular function and to bring solutions in a particular area in which you have capabilities and expertise.

To spell out that you are precisely the person who is capable and motivated to do just that, the body of the **HIGH-IMPACT Cover Letter** consists of three sections:

> ➤ The **Connection Maker** in which you connect with the employer in order to persuade her to read the rest of your letter and look at your resume.

> The *Back-Up* in which you substantiate your qualifications for helping to solve her dilemma by pointing out your relevant experience.

> The *Invite* in which you suggest getting together with her to discuss how you can help her.

## The Connection Maker

The **Connection Maker** is the first paragraph of the **HIGH-IMPACT Cover letter**. Here you briefly discuss why you are writing, including how you learned of the job opening and why you want it in terms of how your experience can benefit the employer.

Professional writers tell us that the two hardest sentences to write are the opening sentence and the closing sentence. The opening statement or paragraph is most crucial in that it must grab the employer's attention to convince her that she should read the rest of your letter and look at your resume. In public speaking, this is sometimes called **the Ho-Hum Crasher!**

The first sentence sums up why you are writing, including the name of the position you are seeking.

Why you are writing may include how you learned of the opening. In telling the employer how you learned of the job, you answer for her the question of how effective her recruiting tools are and perhaps even how her enterprise plays out in the public arena. This is particularly true in answering a newspaper or Internet ad.

When someone known to the employer has recommended that you contact her about a job, especially if it is a business associate of hers, be sure to mention that person's name in the first sentence. Such a recommendation carries a lot of weight. From the employer's perspective, such recommendations are an optimal source of high-performing employees who will be productive on the job.

When applying to a business which has not advertised for the position you are seeking, simply state why you have written and why you think the employer might be interested in what you have to offer in terms of contributing toward meeting mutual goals.

The first sentence is followed by a statement that you believe you are qualified to do the work by virtue of your background and training.

Following are some examples with comments:

> On noting your recent ad in the Anytown Gazette for an assembly supervisor, it seems that my background, knowledge and experience closely fit your requirements. I'd very much like the opportunity to discuss with you how I can contribute to your firm's profitability and growth.

Note that how the applicant learned of the job is stated at the very outset. This tells the employer that he is answering an ad, The second sentence sets the stage for the later ***Invite***  by immediately seeking the opportunity for discussion. The last clause of the second sentence suggests an interest in making a contribution and concern for the employer's "productivity and growth."

The next example is a response for an unadvertised job query and mentions equipment expertise:

> I understand that you have openings for maintenance workers on the Allstate Turnpike. I believe that my extensive background, especially with my experience in construction with the operation and maintenance of large and small equipment will help me be a valuable member of your maintenance team and meet your maintenance goals.

A third example uses a reference as an entree:

> John Noteworthy told me that you are looking for the services of a business manager for Enterprise Associates to reorganize your staff. He suggested that I send along my resume. I have managed a small business for seven years and specialize in conflict resolution and creating an open, friendly, production-stimulating atmosphere. I have heard many good things about Enterprise Associates and would be most honored to become one of your staff.

### *HIGH-IMPACT TIP*

Before using the name of a third party, be sure that you have that person's permission. Not doing so can invite disaster as the third party imparts negative information about you. A letter of recommendation from that person constitutes permission.

A fourth example is an attempt to create a new position for the applicant by providing an in-house service which formerly relied on external sources:

> As a travel consultant, I have worked extensively with your firm in scheduling transportation for your staff. I have been impressed with your operations and believe that, with my broad knowledge of the travel industry, I can make useful contributions as a member of your staff by adding other dimensions and broader insights to your staff travel arrangements.

# The Back-Up

The **Back-up** is the main section of the letter in which you spell out those aspects of your experience and know-how supporting what you said in the first paragraph. These are the proof of the pudding, the information to support your request.

This section can be one to three paragraphs, the length depending on the content of your know-how and experience and its applicability to the job you want.

Here are some examples. The first is from an applicant for assembly supervisor:

> My background includes four years as an assembly supervisor and job training coach for 47 mentally- and physically-handicapped workers. I interviewed them to determine if they could participate, motivated them, helped them work through special problems so that they could increase their productivity. I've also had two years experience as an assembly line worker and many more helping a family-owned business remain productive and profitable.
>
> My specialty is in creating an atmosphere in which worker's satisfaction is reflected in increased quality, efficiency and productivity.

A second example is from a travel consultant:

> As you can see from the enclosed resume, my experience in the travel industry includes working within a major airline company to resolve complaints and maximize customer satisfaction. While with that firm, I also had experience in managing personnel.
>
> I have also worked as a travel consultant arranging and assisting with business and personal vacation planning. I am well acquainted with and adept at using airline computer systems and ticket printers, as well as with current airline requirements.

A third example is from a recent college graduate, here seeking a job as an electronics technician:

> As you can see from the enclosed resume, I've just graduated with an associate degree in electronics from Anytown Community College. While enrolled there, I maintained a 3.8 GPA while working full time.
>
> I have other knowledge that could prove useful to your field service operations. I am an experienced welder and cutter, have gotten this training and experience with the US Army.
>
> I know how to work with and persuade people. I've been working as a telemarketer making cold calls. More recently I've been working as a bartender and developing skills needed to deal effectively and tactfully with even difficult people.
>
> I am flexible, willing to take on a variety of assignments. I'm looking forward to getting the kind of job done that will help your firm hold on to current clients because they're happy about the service they're getting and bring in new clients because of your fine service reputation.
>
> I am willing to relocate and to travel as the job requires. I'll be happy to undergo training to your requirements if that is needed.

## The Invite

The *Invite* is the final paragraph or two in which you specifically set up a means whereby an appointment for an interview can be made.

It is absolutely imperative to end your letter with a request for an interview! That's what you're after! Sales experts speak of the importance of asking for the sale. They point out that many, many sales are lost after otherwise excellent presentations simply because the presenter failed to pose the most important question.

Getting the interview is the purpose of the entire enterprise of preparing both resume and cover letter. Asking for the interview is equivalent to asking for the sale. A successful cover letter, like a successful resume, is the one that gets your prospective employer to talk to you one on one. That interview is your foot inside the door!

Once your foot is there, your resume and cover letter have done their job. Convincing the interviewer that you are the right person for the job is then possible and up to you.

The most proactive approach is to state that you will contact the probable interviewer to set up an appointment for the interview. Your use of a proactive approach suggests to the employer that you take responsibility for getting the job done. Of course, once you have offered to make the contact, it's important to follow up on your letter with the contact. As an example:

> I'd very much like to meet with you to discuss how my skills can contribute to making your firm's services more comprehensive and attractive and to making your operations more effective and efficient.
>
> I can be reached at the above email address and telephone; I'll contact you soon to set up an appointment to discuss how I can be of service to your firm.

It is not always possible to use the proactive approach, particularly when answering blind ads. In that case, you can still ask for the interview, but simply state how you can be reached in order to set it up:

> I would like to meet with you to discuss how I can contribute toward making Anytown Acme's sales staff one of the best in the country. You can reach me to set up an appointment at the above email address and phone or you can call me at work, 555-555-0001.
>
> I'd be proud to be associated with your firm. I am looking forward to meeting with you and talking to you about your plans for your sales team and how I might fit in with those plans. I hope we can do that in the very near future.

# SECTION B

## SOLVING SPECIAL PROBLEMS

# LANDING THAT FIRST JOB

The most daunting task that faces any of us during our lifetime may well be getting started on a career. This means leaving the safety of school behind and entering the unknown and somewhat strange "real world" of business and industry.

Here in the "real world," the rules of engagement are quite different from those you left behind in the academic world. The newness of these rules calls for a corresponding adjustment in your thinking. Emphasis has changed from how well you can learn and your personal development to the value you can contribute toward making the enterprise you are now joining successful.

Correspondingly, one of the most daunting resumes to prepare is the very first for a young applicant just out of school. In most cases, job experience is slight or nonexistent.

In some cases, courses studied in school seem to have little relevance to the job being sought. Often, there seems to be little else in your life history to include in a resume.

Many young jobseekers feel very ill at ease in seeking that first real job. They feel that they are at so much of a tremendous disadvantage competing with older, more experienced workers that they are reluctant to make the attempt.

Set your mind at ease on that score! You are competing in a very different market than the more experienced worker. Your market is in the entry-level job. For the most part, your competition comes from other young people in the same situation.

In point of fact, more experienced workers have much more to fear from you than you from them! As you come in the entry-level door, some of them may find themselves pushed out the door, displaced by *you!*

Employers value young workers for your potential. Fresh out of school, you're much more likely to be attuned to the latest technological innovations developed by universities and taught by other schools in this rapidly changing world than the older worker even just a few years out of school.

You are in the most creative phase of your life with a fresh way of looking at things and, for that reason, much more likely to come up with useful innovations to benefit your employer.

There is the distinct possibility that you have that spark of ability that can be developed into leadership and management skills. You are less likely to be set in your ways or to have developed unfortunate working habits.

Employers have very different expectations for entry-level workers than for more experienced workers. They allow young workers some latitude for inexperience and give them time to make the adjustment from school to work. On the other hand, they will usually not tolerate a lackadaisical attitude or open disrespect for the workplace, superiors, colleagues or clients.

Employers look for a positive attitude toward work in their young applicants, including willingness to take direction. They will question you about your goals to determine if you are likely to have attitudes fostering a forward-moving career from which they can derive benefits.

An older worker competing for an entry-level job, often a woman whose children have grown, is actually at somewhat of a disadvantage in this market. The interviewer will question why you are not further along in your career. You can find further information in the following chapter on changing careers.

The challenge in preparing a resume for a young inexperienced worker lies in drawing from your academic and personal background the quality information that persuades an employer with a special job in mind that you are worth talking to.

One challenge is to make less look like a whole lot more. Consequently, this first resume may well have many features you will drop in later resumes, replacing them with the skills and experience you'll have developed by then. These features include such entries as grade point average, school activities, honor societies and hobbies.

The purpose of this resume, like any other, is to get the interview, not necessarily to land the job. In the course of the interview, it is up to you first to decide if both the job and the employer are for you, that is, if there is a fit between you and the job. If so, your next task is to persuade the employer that you are the one person out of all others he has interviewed who is most worthy of investing his business funds in.

The employer does not expect your resume to look like that of someone with just two years experience. Hiring an entry-level worker is something like handicapping a horse race. The employer is betting on your still unproved potential.

The professional look of your resume and the quality of the information in it may very well make the crucial difference to an employer looking at many poorly-put-together resumes. The mere fact that you've taken the time to research what employers are interested in will speak well for you.

## *Assessing your qualifications*

In assessing your qualifications for an entry-level job, use the process outlined in SECTION A with a few changes in emphasis.

When you have yet to hold down a job, what experience can you possibly have? Usually plenty! The term "experience" can be more broadly interpreted in a first resume to include any school, after school, hobby and extracurricular organizational experience, along with any paying jobs you may have held while going to school. Usually, three to five samplings of your activities most relevant to the job you are seeking are sufficient.

# Relevant work experience

Any work experience is given preferred space over other activities in your resume. Don't be concerned that the job or jobs you hold or have held are of the menial variety. Holding down a job while going to school says something about your steadfastness of purpose. It also suggests that you have been able to satisfy an employer's expectations of you.

- What are the responsibilities of any paying job that you hold or have held?
- What were your achievements on those jobs?

> **HIGH-IMPACT TIP**
>
> If you happen to have been fired from any job while going to school, forget that you ever held that job unless your firing is public knowledge! Going to school is a full-time activity. Don't give former employers an opportunity to provide negative feedback about you! If faced with this situation, take the time to read *Oh! Oh! You were fired! What to do? What to do?*, the fourth and final chapter in this SECTION, which addresses this problem more fully.

# Other relevant experience

- Which class(es) or curriculum or specialized training that you have completed (or will complete by graduation) is or are most relevant to the position you are seeking? Describe the content of the field or lab or classroom experience which suggests that you have useful know-how for the job sought. Describe any special achievement in connection with this experience. Mention any new or specialized technology in which you are competent.

- What were your relevant after-class activities and hobbies? For example, organized sports activities or band membership helps you learn teamwork and leadership skills. Tinkering with cars teaches skill at mechanics. Being part of a debating team teaches communication skills. Helping in a family business teaches business skills and responsibility. The skills may also be listed in the *Hands-On Knowledge of* section of your resume.

All that time you spent hanging out with the guys or gals probably won't help you here. Neither will such hobbies as knitting and crochet or woodworking unless you're seeking a job in a yarn shop or lumberyard.

- What offices did you hold or special responsibilities did you perform? Examples are managing a sports team, serving as a camp counselor, directing a play, assisting in teaching young children or being a class or organizational officer. All of these are very relevant to many jobs.

# *The entry-level HIGH-IMPACT Resume*

A principle difference between an entry-level **HIGH-IMPACT Resume** and one for an experienced worker is arrangement of entries in the lower half of the resume. The shift in order of entries is made to emphasize your strongest selling points as a young worker.

In the **Situation Wanted ad**, state that you are seeking an entry-level job.

The dividing line of the **HIGH-IMPACT Resume**, just below the **Situation Wanted Ad**, subtly directs the eye to the entry just below. This is where you want your strongest selling point.

For a recent graduate, a very strong selling point is your education. Highlight any training that specifically or especially qualifies you for the job you are seeking.

This is true also for recent high-school graduates. The fact of your diploma suggests that you finish what you start. Keep in mind that you are competing for different jobs than the college or university graduate.

If it is high, say at or above 3.25 out of 4, your **Grade Point Average** can be your next entry, followed by any honor societies or other honors to which you have been named. Then follows **Hands-On Knowledge of:** and **Experience:** as outlined in SECTION B.

# CHANGING CAREERS

- Your doctor tells you that continuing in the field in which you've been employed since leaving school is hazardous to your health.

- You've been disabled on the job to the degree that you can no longer perform its duties.

- You've been downsized into early "retirement" but are not yet ready to call it a career. Jobs in your current field are scarce, especially for someone your age.

- Once challenging work is increasingly repetitive and boring with little prospect of challenge or advancement. You're in a deep rut and want out.

- Your career interests are different than they were when you were 22 and you want to try a new line of work.

- You've found yourself in a field you don't really enjoy and in which your talents are minimal.

- Chances for advancement are nonexistent. You must change direction in your field to save your sanity.

- The kids are finally old enough to manage on their own without your constant attention. You want to get going on your "real" career.

- Your skills have been made obsolete and your job eliminated by rapidly changing technology.

- At last you've stumbled onto the kind of work you really want to do for the rest of your career.

These are common reasons for moving from one career path to another very different path. Whatever your reason for taking the leap, the task of seeking a job in a new field when all your experience and most of your qualifications are in your old field can seem like the mother of all challenges.

The challenge of preparing a resume when changing career paths is to find in the sum total of your work and life experience those elements which will be useful to you and your employer in your new capacity. To accomplish this, you first need to understand the skills requirements of the new job you are seeking fully.

## *Identifying needed skills*

Take time to jot down expected responsibilities of the job you're seeking. Make your list as complete as you can. What do you expect to do during a typical day at this job? The lists in **SECTION A** will suggest what can be included. Conversations with a teacher of your new skills or someone already active in your new field will give you further ideas.

Next, determine those skills required by the responsibilities and activities in the rough job description you've just prepared.

Job skills can be categorized in four areas:

➤ Technical skills: information about techniques that have to be known in order to perform the job.

➤ Interpersonal skills: the level and quality of required interaction with other people.

➤ Management skills: know-how to motivate and assess performance, maintain performance levels and needed records and otherwise keep the business solvent.

➤ Work ethic skills: the level of self-motivation or ability to follow directions required.

## Moving up into Management

Stepping up into management from a subordinate job is a career change that requires those adaptations in thinking considered in this chapter. Making the step up into a management position at the same time as making the transition to a new employer is a special category of job change. Management entails a different set of responsibilities and skills from whatever it is that you've been doing up to now.

There are as many paths to management as there are lines of work. Some people, such as MBAs from prestigious colleges or graduates of corporate management training programs, enter the workforce as managers. Lower-level managers more commonly rise through the ranks of the workforce.

Because it is so essential to the operation of any business enterprise, management talent is highly regarded and sought out by employers. Often, the transition in changing careers is to a management position.

Much the same management technique can be applied to any enterprise. Yet, some managers need specialized knowledge: An engineering manager has to know about engineering problem solving. An effective sales manager is up on successful sales principles. Yet, in the management aspect of their work, engineering, sales and other managers all apply the same principles.

If you are interested in moving onto or up the management ladder in your new career, take an added look at those duties you will be required to perform as a manager when preparing the job description for your new dream job. You still need to look at skills you need to perform other aspects of that new position.

## Identifying these skills in your work history

The next step is to determine which of these skills and personal qualities you identified as crucial to the position you're seeking are already part of your repertoire; that is, those you have already developed as a consequence of your work history combined with any leisure time activities relevant to your new career.

Many skills and personal qualities employed in your old job may well prove valuable in your new career. At the very least, any know-how you've developed about setting goals and following through will serve you well in any field.

Once again, just as in seeking your very first job, hobbies and volunteer activities may play an active role to prepare you for your new career. These enable development of job-related skills. Indeed, many discover their new career direction through them.

Hobbies refine motor skills while they develop your knowledge of equipment and materials. Volunteer activities often develop and fine-tune leadership ability and interpersonal skills. They also provide a network of contacts which will surely be an asset in your new position.

## Preparing your HIGH IMPACT Resume

By this time, you've gained a sense of the requirements of the new position and the relevant elements of your experience and qualifications. That yields all the pieces of information needed to prepare your **HIGH IMPACT Resume** using principles laid out in **SECTION A**.

In each part of the resume, highlight those elements of your experience relevant to the position you desire. For example, in the **Situation Wanted Ad**, choose descriptors that support the new position.

The entry immediately below the dividing line immediately below the **Situation Wanted Ad** is likely to catch the resume reviewer's eye once he has read the ad. Therefore, this is the preferred spot for any information you wish to highlight.

For example, if you recently completed courses of study qualifying you for this new line of work, your entry for **Education** should appear here with the recently completed coursework heading the list. Similarly, this is where to place any new pertinent license.

In the ***Hands-on Knowledge of:*** section, list only skills relevant to the new position, particularly if the job is radically different from your old line of work.

When using volunteer experience as qualifications, treat it as another job. For example, a man who wished to make a career of fundraising and served as a volunteer fundraiser for a community agency described his experience as follows:

| VOLUNTEER FUNDRAISING EXPERIENCE: | Fundraising chairman, *Anytown Community Center*, 1990 to 2000: <br> Working with the executive director, led a group of three members in assessing financial needs. Interviewed vendors. Evaluated products. Made cost and profit estimates. Consulted with members for their ideas and concerns. <br> Implemented and led fundraising activity of the Center, determining and evaluating possible fundraising strategies and making appropriate recommendations to the board of directors. <br> In my first year, raised 170% of previous results. Maintained yearly increases in funds raised. |
|---|---|

Rather than using the word "hobby," which has a certain ring of frivolity, experience gained through leisure-time activities can be described more directly in your resume. For example, a client wishing to enter the field of automotive mechanics after a ten-year career in sales had a lifetime hobby of tinkering with and rebuilding the engines of old cars:

| MECHANICAL EXPERIENCE: | Rebuilt and maintained 3 automobile engines. <br> Made repairs as needed. <br> Performed all routine maintenance procedures for family and friends' automobiles. <br> Installed replacement parts as needed. |
|---|---|

In describing past work experience, stress those aspects with direct relevance to your new line of work. For example, if moving into the computer field from waiting tables, highlight your experience in operating the cash register (basically a computer) and maintaining records. If moving into sales from the same job, stress your friendly manner and success in satisfying customers and gaining repeat business.

In both resumes of a one-time food server, both aspects of the old position may be mentioned. Emphasis is created through placement of information and inclusion of supporting details.

In the ***HIGH IMPACT Resume***, the highlighted information is the first to hit the resume reviewer's eye and is described more fully.

# BEATING AGE DISCRIMINATION

*It's just not fair!* Just when you think you have your career on track and your skills and your know-how are at their peak, you find yourself downsized out of a job and the next job very hard to get. All of a sudden, it seems that the very experience that carried you this far up to now no longer has any value for employers.

Age discrimination is very real. Reasons mostly fall into four categories: A major consideration is the high cost of benefits for older employees, especially pensions and health insurance. Statistically, the likelihood of an older worker actually collecting these benefits is much higher.

Second, there is a perception, mistaken or not, that older workers are set in their ways, fixed in the methods of the twenty to forty years past. Consequently, innovative thinking cannot be expected from them.

Some employers actively seek to employ an exclusively young staff under the belief that youth attracts business. They support this by pointing to demographics. Young people make up a larger proportion of the buying public.

Fourth is the likelihood that the applicant won't hold the job long enough for the employer to recoup hiring expenses through the applicant's performance on the job. This is particularly true of applicants near retirement age. As soon as the employee is fully trained, she will want to retire, leaving the employer to go through the entire hassle of hiring yet again.

Working in your favor is the perception that older workers are more reliable and have a better work ethic.

Age discrimination takes place very early in the hiring process. It usually happens during the preliminary review of submitted resumes, long before anyone is invited to an interview. Information provided in a resume is routinely used to disqualify who do not fit the implied age profile the employer has designated for each job to be filled. The resume of an obviously older worker is simply bypassed and eliminated.

When this happens, proving age discrimination in court is virtually impossible. Those employers who discriminate for any reason have learned well how to leave few tracks of their discrimination.

The range of ages acceptable to an employer varies with the employer and type of job. As a rule of thumb, a whole lot of employers regard age 40 as the age of diminishing returns and skyrocketing costs for retaining an employee.

Age discrimination can be beaten, or at least neutralized. As you approach and pass age 40, make an intensive review of your whole job search package (resume, cover letter, letters of recommendation, certificates and commendations). Are you running up red flags of advancing age, thereby giving resume reviewers reasons to disqualify you?

Red flags include:

> ➤ ***Dates of employment:*** If these exceed 20 years out of high school or 15 years out of college, you're very probably getting close to age 40 if you haven't already passed it. Resume reviewers can do the math to figure this out.

To avoid raising this red flag, sound strategy is to omit all dates from your resume. You can put the correct dates on your employment application. Once you've obtained the interview, age discrimination is much easier to prove. Many resumes crossing employers' desks every day omit dates. Omitted dates to not raise a red flag.

Exceptions to this strategy are dates of recent accomplishment. For example, if within the past five or so years, you completed training to upgrade your skills to meet the requirements of the job you're seeking, by all means put in and even highlight the date when you were awarded the degree or certificate. A recent graduation date suggests to the resume reviewer that you are a young applicant. Thus, it works in your favor.

Other exceptions include recent licenses or honors relevant to the position you are seeking.

> ➤ ***Way too much experience:*** When you show 35 years of job experience by listing many jobs and promotions, a resume reviewer will come to conclusions about your probable age and disqualify you.

A resume is not a work history. There is no need to record every detail of every job you have ever held on a resume. You need not even include every job. Only those aspects of past jobs relevant to the job you are seeking need to be described.

A high-level manager from a major firm brought in his resume. In its two pages were descriptions of every job he had ever held within that firm in considerable detail. (Two pages already say that way too much information is being provided.) His resume started with his entry-level job as a junior accountant and progressed through some five promotions to his current very high-level management position.

Although his considerable experience indicated a very high degree of management expertise that had to be invaluable to any firm that hired him, this resume disqualified him for future employment. By describing all those jobs, he highlighted his probable age for a grateful resume reviewer.

Moreover, far too much information listed was irrelevant to the job he was seeking. He was not applying for an entry-level job as a junior accountant or in lower management. These jobs require very different skills from the duties of vice-president for finance he's so well qualified to fill. Therefore, information on those jobs is neither pertinent to the job being sought nor likely to generate interest from a resume reviewer. Instead, it simply pegged him in the high-risk age group.

His ***HIGH-IMPACT Resume*** focused only on his last two positions and his considerable contributions to the success of the firm in those two positions. It underlined his mastery of those issues important to high management.

> ➤ *Age references in collateral materials:* Examples are letters of recommendation mentioning how many years you filled the job or the writer has known you. Others are certificates or commendations with dates on them that take you out of the desired age range.

Examine all collateral materials enclosed with a resume carefully to ensure that they don't disqualify you because of age.

A plant manager whose job disappeared because of a plant shutdown brought in a letter of recommendation from his former boss. It laid out the boss's high esteem for his employee's many wonderful character values and job accomplishments in glowing detail.

Unfortunately, the second sentence of its very first paragraph *disqualified* its subject from consideration for any further employment on the level he was seeking, "Mr. X has given us outstanding service for more than 45 years." Very few resume reviewers would read past that sentence before putting the resume on the reject pile. This applicant is too close to retirement age to invest company funds in him.

### HIGH-IMPACT TIP

When a letter of recommendation suggests that you are an older worker, ask the writer to have it retyped on appropriate stationery without that information and to sign it again. Most will be happy to do so because they have a positive attitude toward you and genuinely want to help you.

If that isn't possible, simply file the letter for use when your spirits need a lift. Leave it out of your resume packet.

Once an interview is secured, you'll have the opportunity to convince an employer that you have a great deal to contribute to the success of his business precisely because of your wisdom and experience. Make the most of it by being prepared to meet his likely objections outlined at the beginning of this chapter.

# OH! OH! YOU WERE FIRED! WHAT TO DO? WHAT TO DO?

So, you were fired! You were dismissed from your most recent job, not for lack of work, not for downsizing, not for the end of a contract, but sadly because your employers found you or your performance very unsatisfactory.

What a spot! What to do? What to do?

Understandably, you are very anxious. You wonder, "Is this the end of my career? How can I possibly get another job? How can I get any employer to even talk to me?"

Take heart! This difficult experience may very well be the beginning of your career! It may be the boot in the pants you needed to convince you that it's time to get your priorities in order.

Your first priority is to take a good look at what really happened so that you can make the changes that'll insure that something like this won't happen again.

Many, many people who have been fired have moved on into thriving, productive and satisfying careers. You're the one who can make sure that happens for you!

## *What really happened to you?*

Just as employers come in all sizes and shapes, there are both legitimate and phony reasons for dismissing employees. Take the time to assess the whole situation you're in, including the events leading to your dismissal from your employer's point of view as well as your own. It will help you choose an effective strategy tailor-made for you.

As often stated on these pages, there is no one-size-fits-all strategy for finding a job. There are general principles that usually get good results. After looking at the reasons why employees are dismissed, we'll look at factors to take into consideration in designing your personal strategy.

How about it? Were you dismissed with good reason? Or were you enmeshed in a stressful situation over which you had little or no control? Or was it a mixture of the two? How much did you contribute to driving the situation out of control? Truthful answers will steer you toward better choices.

***A new job is always an opportunity to make a new beginning!*** What changes are you willing to make in your on-the-job performance and behaviors in order to put your career on a success track?

Legitimate reasons for dismissing employees include:

> You consistently refused to follow reasonable or established work rules, such as through habitual tardiness or taking unauthorized days off.

> Your behavior was flagrantly inappropriate to the workplace, such as engaging in foul language, wearing inappropriate dress, or even engaging in inappropriate sexual intercourse in an inappropriate place (it has happened!).

> You were insolent to a superior, coworkers or clients.

> You were caught red-handed in dishonesty.

> You failed to maintain confidentiality.

Less valid reasons for dismissal might be:

> Your superior has a difficult personality and made unreasonable demands on staff that you could not ethically meet.

> A new superior or a new owner was brought in who wanted your job for a former associate, family member or friend.

> You blew the whistle on unsafe, unauthorized or even illegal practices which brought about retaliation in the form of job dismissal.

> A superior or coworker caused the trouble and you took the fall.

> Your employer discovered that you were looking for a job elsewhere.

Businesses differ tremendously in the workplace environment they create. Attitudes of owners and top managers influence the workplace climate greatly. The level of trust that management has for workers is reflected in the workplace atmosphere. Your job search provides a fresh opportunity to shop around for a workplace environment which will nurture *YOU!*

## What to do? Assess your situation!

Once your self-assessment is complete and you've begun to take appropriate steps to readjust those attitudes and behaviors which stand between you and job success, you're ready to organize your job search. The work you've just done in assessing your situation will give you a start on the process.

Beyond doubt, the key factor in making strategy decisions in your situation is precisely the one beyond your control: ***What is your former employer likely to say about you to your prospective employers?*** Just how damaging is that likely to be to your chances of getting that crucial initial interview, much less your chances of being hired?

Do prospective employers check your job references? **YOU BET THEY DO!** Most do it very early, even before deciding to talk to you.

If you parted on good terms with your former employer or the assessment of both you and your work is likely to be at least neutral, you have breathing room. You can safely use most elements of job search strategy discussed in earlier chapters with relative peace of mind. Still, be prepared with positive responses to your interviewer's questions about the circumstances surrounding your firing.

Many companies, especially larger corporations, have adopted a policy of merely confirming that former employees have worked for them and the dates of employment. They do this to avoid lawsuits and undue attention from state and federal regulatory agencies.

Even then, prospective employers sometimes have other contacts within your former workplace, people who can give them the unvarnished off-the-record version of what really happened and what sort of employee you were. Be prepared for such surprises!

If the reasons for your dismissal are legitimate from the employer's view, it's undoubtedly time ***now*** to change your thinking and behavior before moving on to another job and another failure. Expect your interviewer to probe this in depth and to pay close attention to your responses.

If you can't keep up with the work or it bores you, ***why stay in that line of work?*** This is an excellent time to train for a different, more satisfying career. Financial aid is often available. Coincidentally, going back to school puts a useful buffer between you and the failed job experience in that next search for a job.

Failure to get along with other people is the number one cause for job failure. No employer wants an employee who refuses to make an effort to get along with superiors, coworkers and clients. Such an employee disrupts the workplace and, thereby, significantly reduces staff productivity. These disruptions create a hostile workplace environment which drives customers away. Thus, they have a very negative impact on the bottom line. Resulting low staff morale actually can put a company out of business!

If the problem was your attitude, that's something only you can change! Get the chip off your shoulder! Professional counseling may help you get at the root of your negative attitudes so that you can overcome them. A more accommodating approach will move you much further toward your goals.

Similarly, if you were caught in dishonesty, you can learn from the experience. You have the opportunity to make a new start. Once again, professional counseling may help you overcome the defective thinking that got you in such a mess.

If, on the other hand, your dismissal came about because of a prevailing negative climate in your former workplace or unfair practices of your former employer, count yourself lucky to be out of a very repressive and unproductive environment. You may even have learned enough from the experience to know what to look for in order not to get into such an employment situation next time around.

Owners and managers of smaller businesses are often simply content to have the source of their irritation—in this case, you—off their premises and out of their lives. Unless the dismissed employee has been particularly obnoxious, dishonest or disruptive, nothing will be said to other employers. As often as not, business managers are embarrassed by such situations and don't want it to be known that they made such a disastrous business decision in selecting an employee. They figure it's bad for business.

Some employers may be so mad that they cannot contain what they say. Others feel it is their moral duty to protect other businesses from you. Still others may be so spiteful that, given the least opportunity, they will torpedo any move by a former employee they don't like. The scenario that applies in your case should figure into your job search strategy. You probably have some sense of your former employer's attitude and mode of operation.

There are clues to be picked up from the circumstances surrounding your dismissal. You may have even witnessed what happened to former colleagues under similar circumstances.

## What to do? Devise a strategy

Effective strategy takes the total picture into account. It focuses on assets while minimizing liabilities. A positive focus can do much to minimize liabilities.

How can you focus on assets? What is the total package you have to offer your next employer? What special education or qualifications? What skills? What job experiences and achievements? These are vital to any effective job search strategy. They are even more important for you.

How can you minimize liabilities? There are two strategies for dealing with potential negative feedback from a former employer: circumvent it entirely or neutralize it as much as possible.

Circumventing potential negative feedback is preferred when circumstances permit. In this strategy, you essentially "forget" that you ever worked for a particular employer. Omit all references from job search materials, including your resume, cover letters and letters of recommendation. Bring up nothing at all related to that job in employment interviews.

This course of action is not without risk. Be prepared to deal with any questions about your dismissal that may come up, including why you omitted any references to it.

When do circumstances permit "forgetting" about a job? Whenever the omission doesn't raise red flags for the employer. Examples are:

- You held the job from which you were dismissed less than a year and left your last previous job a year or so ago or less. Especially in a tight labor market, it can take some folks that long to find a job.

- You are young, less than two years out of school and this was your first job on leaving school. Once more, in a tight labor market, it can easily take some folks that long to land their first job in their chosen field.

- You held down the job while going to school. Not holding a job while in school full time will not be questioned.

- You have established significant other experience or training since leaving the job from which you were dismissed. This gives you a buffer to deflect curiosity. You have something else to feature and talk about.

### *HIGH IMPACT TIP*

When omitting a job from your resume, be wary of time gaps between jobs. An observant resume reviewer will pick this up and either screen you out or ask you about the gap. If there is a large gap, more than a year, leave all dates of employment off your resume.

When is it unwise to "forget" a job? When the red flags will be there no matter what you do. Some examples are:

- You worked for several years for the employer who dismissed you. Here, you are between a rock and a hard place. The gap of omission raises the wrong kinds of questions. Employers tend to think that anyone unemployed for some time is unemployable; there must be something wrong with that person.

- Your significant experience or skills are associated with the work you did with that employer. If you want to claim the experience or skill on your resume, you have to include the job.

- Your firing is public knowledge. There were news stories about it (as with the head of a public agency).

- You were accused, even convicted, of a crime other than a minor traffic infraction; there are records of this. In the resume reviewer's eyes, omission of such information is tantamount to lying and you are demonstrating a lack of trustworthiness. Better be up-front about it so that it doesn't rear up to destroy you at some later time.

When you cannot "forget" a job, there are a number of steps you can take to minimize the potential damage. Your aim here is to create the opportunity to present the case for your employment before a bad reference presents the opposing case. To put it another way, you must secure the opportunity for the interview without giving your former employer the opportunity to see to it that you are not interviewed.

A widely used device for doing just this is not to release the name of your former employer until the interview. A notation, "name released on negotiation" replaces the name of your former employer on your resume. This technique is commonly used by job seekers who do not want their present employer to know that they are job-hunting. Some employers routinely fire employees just for looking for another job. Consequently, the phrase will not raise a red flag.

### HIGH IMPACT TIP

If you can, use the name of someone other than the manager who fired you as your reference within that company. If might be an earlier supervisor with the same firm, preferably one who gave you good reviews. It might be a former colleague with some standing in the company with whom you have a good relationship or did an outstanding piece of work. Be sure to inform your new reference and ask permission to use his name in order to avoid unpleasant surprises.

### HIGH IMPACT TIP

Better yet, ask the person you choose as a reference to write a letter of recommendation for you. Check the letter over before forwarding it to make sure that it contains no damaging information. If it's likely to make a positive impression and persuade an employer to talk to you, enclose a copy along with your resume and cover letter. This will create a positive spin to soften any later negative input. It could even forestall the telephone call for information about you to the person with the negative spin.

A second letter of recommendation from a different employer will reinforce the positive spin. More than two or three such letters will probably not be read.

When filling out an application, omit the name of the employer you've "forgotten." Include the name of the employer withheld "until negotiations." Those negotiations are your interview. Where it asks for your supervisor's name, if you can do so truthfully, give the name of the person you asked to vouch for you, even if he was not your most recent supervisor.

# *That crucial interview*

***PREPARE WELL FOR YOUR INTERVIEW.*** It is much more crucial for you than for any other applicant.

Make your objective to present everything about you and your background in the most favorable light you can muster. Keep that objective firmly in mind as you go through the interview. Keep bringing the conversation back to your positives whenever you can.

Take special care in how you present the circumstances around your dismissal. This will make or break the impression you leave and your chances for employment. Be straightforward, truthful and brief. Most especially, **don't make accusations against or assassinate the character of your former boss**, even if he truly is a prime candidate for the *Worst Boss of the Century!* Any diatribe against a former employer makes *you* come across as a troublemaker and a poor employment risk.

The person interviewing you is not there as a judge to decide your "case" against a former employer. In any case, your ex-boss is not on trial. **YOU are!**

## HIGH IMPACT TIP

If you have bad feelings toward your former workplace, colleagues or superior, talk them over with a counselor, your pastor, your friends or your family, ***NOT*** with your interviewer. She is not there to hear your sad story or to counsel you.

Your interviewer is there for just one purpose, to assess whether you are likely to make a contribution to the productivity of the workplace and, so, are worth the investment in hiring and training you. ***That's all!*** That's also what you are there to show. ***Don't let yourself be sidetracked!***

Yes, she may listen and sympathize. But all the while she's thinking "How fast can I get this loser out of my office?" *Pity-the-poor-victim* approach will not cut it with most employers. They're not in business to provide social services to employees. What's more, they don't want or need professional victims on their staff. Such employees are unlikely to be productive and very likely to cause problems. Nor will *"Just give me a chance!"* win points for you, despite all the romantic fiction to the contrary. Those novels were not written by employers or their interviewers. A much better strategy is to show the employer that there is little risk in hiring you.

## HIGH IMPACT TIP

If a mistake on your part led to your dismissal, take responsibility for it! Talk about what you learned from the experience and what you have done or will do to avoid similar mistakes in the future. Then, move the conversation back to your assets.

Believe me, you will come through with shining colors AND A JOB and move forward with your career.

# SECTION C

## SAMPLE RESUMES & COVER LETTERS

These illustrative resumes and cover letters are adapted from those ***HIGH-IMPACT Resumes*** and ***HIGH-IMPACT Cover Letters prepared by the author for actual clients***. They were selected to illustrate various types of jobs and career management situations.

Names and crucial facts are altered to protect the privacy of clients. Any resemblance to names of real people, firms or organizations is purely coincidental except for national organizations for which the applicant was a volunteer, not an employee.

You'll note that though the general format is the same for all these examples, the format allows for variations in style.

# Resume of Andrew L. Dealer

124 Marigold Lane     *     Anytown, Anystate 11111     *     (555) 555-5555

Personable, dynamic, friendly, outgoing, energetic and hardworking
experienced **Car Dealership Sales Manager**,
a proven performer with a track record of accomplishment, an innovative profit-conscious team leader who knows how to motivate his team to pearl performance, a knowledgeable objective organizer who has an instinct for the right decision at the crucial time, and an adaptable teamwork-oriented communicator, open to suggestion, who knows how to handle people who are upset and bring about a mutually satisfactory problem resolution, seeks to turn a profit for an aggressive, dynamic, quality, forward-moving firm.

=*=*=*=*=*=*=*=*=*=*=*=*=*=*=*=*=*=*=*=*=*=*=*=*=*=*=*=*=*=*=*=*=*=*=*=*=*=*=*=*=*=*=

| | |
|---|---|
| HANDS-ON KNOWLEDGE OF: | All aspects of sales and sales management, including setting targets, qualifying buyers and closing sales.<br>Negotiating with customers, vendors and corporate suppliers.<br>Interviewing, hiring, evaluating, motivating and dismissing employees.<br>Training employees and developing training programs.<br>Inventory management, basic accounting and computer operations.<br>Cost cutting and profit enhancement. |
| SALES MANAGEMENT EXPERIENCE: | Sales manager, *Deluxe Lexus*, Smalltown, Yourstate<br>Oversaw the activities of 14 employees in all aspects of the sales operations, including the new and used care departments. Increased profit through floor plan. Raised car sales average of 45 to 50 cars per month to 100 to 110 cars per month. Set sales records each month. Raised gross profit per unit more than $750.<br>Drew up monthly sales forecasts to generate sales and control expenses of the sales operations, Led weekly sales meetings.<br>Responsible for referencing products and matching presold orders.<br>Interviewed, hired, trained, evaluated, scheduled and dismissed employees. Oversaw training and motivation of staff.<br><br>General Sales Manager, *Gold Motor Sales*, Anytown, Anystate<br>Oversaw the activities of up to 12 sales personnel, a business manager and a lot attendant in all aspects of new and used Toyota cars. Increased sales from 30 to 40 to 60 to 70 cars per month realizing an increase of more than $400 per unit in gross profit.<br>Responsible for annual sales planning and meeting sales goals. Drew up monthly sales forecasts to generate sales and control expenses. Led manager variable meetings among department heads.<br><br>Sales manager, *Extraordinary Motor Sales*, Yourtown, Anystate<br>Oversaw the activities of 8 sales personnel, a business manager and a lot attendant in all aspects of the sale of new GM and used cars. Increased income per deal average by more than $500 without raising car prices. Realized $10,000 in savings per year by reducing stock of less popular models.<br>Developed training program and trained staff. |
| EDUCATION: | Computer and business courses, *Anytown Technical College*<br>Various GM and Toyota sales and product training courses<br>Management training, *Buick Vision Center*<br>Lease Link Training, versions 4.0 and 4.5 |

# Resume of Joel L. Jobseeker

**2020 Any Avenue   *   Anytown, Anystate 11111   *   555-555-5555**

Versatile, conscientious, self-motivated, injury-free and responsible
experienced **Welder-Fabricator and Heavy Equipment Operator**
certified in unlimited thickness plate stick welding, a reliable thorough producer who enjoys taking on a variety of challenges, a safety-conscious achiever who turns in a superior performance with minimal supervision, takes pride in turning out quality work and takes care of equipment, and a team worker with a broad range of technical knowhow who works well with other workers, seeks to put his skills to work for a quality, forward moving firm.

ʭʭʭʭʭʭʭʭʭʭʭʭʭʭʭʭʭʭʭʭʭʭʭʭʭʭʭʭʭʭʭʭʭʭʭʭʭʭʭʭʭʭʭʭʭʭʭʭʭʭʭʭʭʭʭʭʭʭ

**CERTIFICATION:** Unlimited thickness plate stick welding.

**LICENSE:** Anystate chauffeur's license.

**HANDS-ON KNOWLEDGE OF:**
Welding and fabrication: sheet pile assembly, hard surfacing arc gouging
Blueprint reading.
Large equipment and truck operation.
Mechanical and electrical systems.
Safety precautions and procedures.

**WELDING/ LARGE EQUIPMENT FABRICATION & OPERATION EXPERIENCE:**

Welder/Fabricator, *Jones Quarry*, July2020 to present:
Perform various assignments associated with operation of a quarry and stone-crushing firm, as required.
Weld and fabricate sheet pile. As a member of crew, cut, line up, weld, build framework and install sheet piling. Setup and install warp-drive system.
Install conveyor belt system and hydraulic tanks.
Operate crane and boom truck. Rig, load and move and unload trucks. tripper car to load barges with stone.

Ironworker/welder/fabricator: *Anytown Steel Fabrication*, March 2018 to July 2020:
Served as member of crew to construct Butler buildings. Welded and fabricated from blueprints and diagrams. Poured footers and piers. Erected steel substructure Welded and constructed container vessels. Performed other similar tasks.

**OTHER EXPERIENCE:**
Various positions, *Anytown Corp*, March 2016 to March 2018:
Performed various duties for an auto parts subcontractor. Handled stock. Performed final quality check on finished parts Operated presses to form Panels and presses for cars and trucks.

**EDUCATION:**
Graduate, *Anytown High School*, vocational electricity program.
Welding & fabrication, *Anytown Community College*. 2014-15

# Resume of Patricia Personnel, SPHR

222 Main Street   *   Anytown, Anystate 11111   *   (555) 555-5555
patper@fiction.net

Personable, dynamic, dependable, hardworking, flexible and approachable
experienced **Human Resources Manager**,
a Certified Senior Professional Resources Manager
with superior communication skills, a hands-on results achiever who sees what has to be done and does
it, an innovative problem solver with an orderly mind who does not hesitate to tackle new and
difficult challenges and is always looking for ways to do things better, and a conflict resolution
specialist who works well under pressure, excels at calming people and situations down and
maintains good relations with staff and management seeks to put her skills to work
for a quality, forward moving enterprise.

-=-=-=-=-=-=-=-=-=-=-=-=-=-=-=-=-=-=-=-=-=-=-=-=-=-=-=-=-=-=-=-=-=-=-=-=-=-=-=-=-=-=-=-=-=-=-=-=-

| | |
|---|---|
| EDUCATION: | BA, Management, *Anystate University*, 2010<br>Certificate, Senior Professional Resources Management, SHRM, 2011<br>Certificate, Labor Relations, *Anystate University*, 2012<br>Certificate, Preventing Workplace Harassment, *EEOC*, 2010<br>Certificate, Human Resources Management, *Employers Research Council*, 2013 |
| HONOR: | *Anytown YWCA Woman of Achievement* Merit Award Winner, 2015 |
| HANDS-ON KNOWLEDGE OF: | All aspects of Human Resources Management, including personnel policy development, employee records maintenance, performance review, benefits administration, workman's compensation, personnel selection and compliance with federal and state law<br>Microsoft Office Programs including Word, Excel, and Powerpoint.<br>Managing and motivating employees.<br>Training employees and developing training programs. |
| HUMAN RESOURCES MANAGEMENT EXPERIENCE: | Human Resources Manager, *Anytown Public Library*, 2011 to present<br><br>Direct the activities of 3 staff members in all aspects of human resources management for up to 135 employees in the main library and five branch libraries. Created department and developed. Implement and update first written personnel policies for the library. Oversee personnel files management, benefits administration and workman's Compensation, Introduced and maintain computer-automated personnel functions, Computer data and record keeping.<br>Responsible for recruitment, interviewing and selection of personnel. Insure Compliance with federal and state regulations. Oversee safety training. Prepare and Submit department budgets.<br>With assistant director, resolve grievances, Serve as member of negotiating Team for employee relations in a union environment.<br>Developed and implement attendance improvement program which reduced Absenteeism by more than 20%. Negotiated with union for employee participation.<br>Developed performance review program and trained department managers to review policies, procedures and record keeping.<br>Developed and administer training programs for management, including sexual Harassment prevention and family medical leave act provisions. |

# Resume of Michael P. Manager
1555 State Street    *    Anytown, Anystate    *    (555) 555-5555
mikemanager@fiction.net

Versatile, dynamic, creative, knowledgeable and hard-working
experienced **Professional Business Manager**,
a cost-conscious results getter who knows how to streamline procedures for optimal efficiency and
effectiveness, a gifted trainer/motivator who knows how to inspire staff to peak performance,
a problem solver who works through people to find viable solutions that staff will implement,
and a leader of thorough integrity who cares about people, deals with them fairly with humor
and established good working relationships, seeks to put his strengths to work
for a quality, forward moving firm.

%%%%%%%%%%%%%%%%%%%%%%%%%%%%%%%%%%%%%%%%%%%%%%%%%%%%%%%%%%

**HANDS-ON KNOWLEDGE OF:**   All aspects of effective management, including interviewing, training, motivating and evaluating personnel.
Forecasting; developing budgets and policies.
Analyzing business data and procedures.
Cost effectiveness procedures.
Negotiating with vendors.
All aspects of accounting and marketing, including use of computers.

**BUSINESS MANAGEMENT EXPERIENCE:**   Director, patient accounts, *Anytown Hospital*

Directed the activities of 17 employees in all aspects of processing patient accounts for an 80-bed hospital. Oversaw accounts receivable, patient accounting, credits and collections, patient registration and switchboard.
Realized $15,000,000 in collections annually.
Interviewed, hired, trained, scheduled and evaluated staff.
Developed cash forecasts. Analyzed receivables to determine problems and find solutions. Developed policies and procedures.
Developed departmental budget and insured compliance. Developed cash forecasts. Analyzed receivables to determine problems and find solutions. Developed policies and procedures.
Purchased capital equipment. Negotiated with vendors.
Reduced accounts receivable to net 54 days, improving cash flow.
Implemented an electronic billing system.

Business Manager, *Yourtown Hospital*:

Directed the activities of 37 employees in all pets of processing patient accounts for a 200-bed hospital, as above. Realized $36,000,000 in collections annually. Established outpatient and emergency registration department, consolidating activities into one function.

**EDUCATION:**   B.A., business administration with emphasis on management and marketing, *University of Bigtown*.
A.A., business administration, *Anytown Community College*.

# RESUME OF JANE E. STUDENT
555 Third Avenue   *   Anytown, Anystate 11111   *   (555) 555-5555   *   jestudent@fiction.net

Warm, friendly, dependable, imaginative and adaptive hard-working **Elementary Educator**, a recent graduate certified by Anystate to teach, an effective communicator who works well with children and adults and knows how to maintain discipline, defuse tense situations and work effectively with and motivate difficult personalities, and a creative innovator who works to create a friendly growth-stimulating atmosphere, seeks a challenging position with a quality institution of learning.

o=oo=oo=oo=oo=oo=oo=oo=oo=oo=oo=oo=oo=oo=oo=oo=oo=oo=oo=oo=oo=oo=o

| | |
|---|---|
| EDUCATION: | B.Sc., elementary education, *Anystate University*, 2022<br>Graduated *Summa Cum Laude*. |
| TEACHING CERTIFICATE: | Anystate Elementary Education, grade 1 through 8. |
| ELEMENTARY EDUCATION EXPERIENCE: | 3rd grade student teacher, *Eastfield Academy*, Yourtown, (student teaching assignment, 10 weeks):<br>Assisted in teaching inner city children. Assisted in preparing children for Christmas pageant.<br><br>2nd grade observer, *Eastfield Elementary School*, Yourtown (methods training assignment, 5 weeks):<br>Observed and assisted in teaching inner city children. |
| OTHER EXPERIENCE: | Waitress, *Alice's Restaurant*, Anytown, 2018 to 2021 (summers while on vacation from college):<br>Attended to needs of restaurant and bar guests. |
| VOLUNTEER EXPERIENCE: | Assistant leader, Girl Scout Brownie troop: 2018 to 2020<br>Member, College of Education Council, *Anystate University*, 2020 to 2022<br>Member, Strolling Players Society, *Anystate University*, 2019-2022 |
| HONORS: | Honor roll, 2017-2022: Maintained a 3.86 GPA.<br>National Merit Scholar<br>Member, *National Educational Honor Society* |

# Resume of Sharon N. Goodworker

444 State Road   *   Anytown, Anystate 11111   *   (555) 555=5555   *   <u>sharonng@fiction.net</u>

Personable, efficient, versatile and highly professional experienced
**Office Manager / Computer Applications Specialist**,
an innovative achiever knowledgeable about banking, finance, and all aspects of office management
with a keen interest in effective management, a problem solver with outstanding
people skills who knows how to motivate employees and interact effectively
with the public, and a registered notary public seeks to put her know-how
to work for a quality forward-moving firm.

-=-=-=-=-=-=-=-=-=-=-=-=-=-=-=-=-=-=-=-=-=-=-=-=-=-=-=-=-=-=-=-=-=-=-=-=-=-=-=-=-=-=-=-

| | |
|---|---|
| **HANDS-ON KNOWLEDGE OF:** | Registered Notary Public<br>Banking and money-handling procedures.<br>Computer applications. Data entry, word processing, OFFICE, RAMIS<br>Accounts receivable<br>Customer contact and interaction |
| **OFFICE MANAGEMENT EXPERIENCE:** | Assistant credit manager, *Acme Widgets Co.*, October 2019 to present:<br><br>Oversaw the activities of 10 employees in maintaining computer records of distributions of 425 varieties of widgets to wholesalers and retailers. Supervise data entry and generation of records.<br>Train employers to system, Wrote training manual. Assist in maintaining attendance records. Resolve problems as needed.<br>Process daily cash receipts, taking in some $2,000,000 per month. Implement collection procedures on bad checks.<br>Implemented data entry system. Developed data entry functions into an operational unit.<br>Assisted in installation of open-item receivables system. Served on team to review system and recommend changes. |
| **BANKING EXPERIENCE:** | Various positions, *Neighborhood Credit Union*, October 2015 to January 2019:<br>Credit assistant: drew up paperwork to support loan applications and title transfers. Filed liens as required. Performed bookkeeping, using computer.<br>Served on a team to determine which computer to purchase.<br>Share draft clerk: Coordinated check processing with *Chase Manhattan Bank*. Counseled customers in reconciling accounts,<br>Teller: Performed various money transactions and clerical duties. Trained two new tellers. |
| **EDUCATION:** | Business administration, *Academia College*, 2018 to present.<br>Banking and accounting, *American Institute for Banking*.<br>Introduction to RAMIS, *Center for Advanced Software*, Chicago |
| **MEMBERSHIP:** | *National Association for Female Executives* |

# Resume of Arnold D. Exec

2020 Account Avenue   *   Anytown, Anystate 11111   *   (555) 555-5555   *   adexec505@fiction.net

Enterprising, dynamic, versatile, insightful, hard-driving and hardworking experienced
**Business Projects & Properties Developer / Manager**,
an energetic results getter who pulls his weight on a management team, an aggressive entrepreneur who sees the big picture and knows how to structure and finance commercial packages and develop properties, and a born manager who knows how to motivate, seeks business-building responsibilities with an aggressive forward-moving firm.

00=00=00=00=00=00=00=00=00=00=00=0000=00=00=00=00=00=00=00=00=00=00=00=00=00

| | |
|---|---|
| HANDS-ON KNOWLEDGE OF: | Commercial and residential property management and development<br>Relevant state and federal requirements.<br>Development of financial packages and commercial deals.<br>Bankruptcy management. |
| EXECUTIVE MANAGEMENT EXPERIENCE: | Vice-President/ area supervisor for properties and restaurant management, *D. D. Exec and Sons, Inc.*, September 2015 to February 2022:<br><br>Directed real estate and restaurant chain operation for a family owned business that owns and operates a broad spectrum of commercial and residential properties. Supervised chain of six *Faststeak Restaurants*. Hired, trained and evaluated management personnel. Insured operations were profitable and implemented corrective actions to maintain profitability. Ensured that OSHA and other laws were observed. Oversaw merit raises for employees. Built restaurants from scratch. Acquired land. Obtained necessary permits. Engaged and oversaw construction firm.<br>Supervised real estate transactions of up to $500,000. Acquired properties, developed and sold or leased them. Put necessary financing together.<br><br>Assistant branch manager, *ABC Financial Services, Inc.*, July 2010 to August 2015: Made loans to customers for purchase of real estate: Obtained credit references initiated loan applications, referred for approval; followed up for collections and oversaw bankruptcies. |
| MEMBERSHIPS: | *Ultra Country Club*<br>*Anytown Rotary Club,*<br>*Anycounty Chamber of Commerce* |
| EDUCATION: | B.A., pre-law, *Anystate University*, 2006<br>Certificate, real estate, *Academia College*, 2007<br>Certificate studies, finance (2 quarters), *Yourtown University*, 2009<br>Certificate, consumer lending programs, *ABC*, 2009 |

# Resume of Irving Inventory

**317 Resume Drive** * **Anytown, Anystate** * **(555) 555-5555** * **IRVINGV@fiction.net**

Versatile, adaptable, dynamic, thorough, dependable, dedicated and highly motivated
experienced **OPERATIONS / PRODUCTION MANAGER**,
a team builder with outstanding organizational skills who knows how to direct and motivate
employees to optimum performance, a results-oriented achiever with a good memory
who pays attention to details that make the difference and a quick study with a strong work
ethic who enjoys the challenge of finding effective ways of getting the job done
seeks to put his dedication and management knowhow
to work for an aggressive and forward-moving firm.

%%%%%%%%%%%%%%%%%%%%%%%%%%%%%%%%%%%%%%%%%%%%%%%%%%%%

| | |
|---|---|
| **HANDS-ON KNOWLEDGE OF:** | All aspects of operations management.<br>*Just in Time* procedures and philosophy.<br>Direction and motivation of union and nonunion employees.<br>Interviewing, hiring, dismissing and disciplining employees.<br>Training employees.<br>Troubleshooting and problem resolution techniques.<br>Inventory control and purchasing.<br>Banking and money handling procedures.<br>Computer programs: *Word, Word Perfect, Excel* and *A&400 System*. |
| **OPERATIONS MANAGEMENT EXPERIENCE:** | Operations manager, *Acme Transportation*, Anytown, 2018 to 2022:<br><br>Directed the activities of up to 68 production warehouse employees over three shifts in a 152,000 square foot facility in an automotive parts sequencing operation for *Just in Time* delivery to Ford. Built up sequencing operations from 2 to 17 items over a four-year period.<br>Interviewed, hired, trained, scheduled, disciplined and fired employees.<br>Gathered payroll data and entered it into computer.<br>Using mainframe computer programs, monitored production rates entered by employees using scan guns. Transferred data to a spreadsheet.<br>Troubleshot production difficulties and resolved mechanical and human relations difficulties.<br>Tool inventory and determined purchasing needs. Monitored shipping and receiving to ensure correct on-time loading and that everything ordered was accounted for and undamaged.<br>Interfaced with customers as needed to ascertain needs. |
| **BANKING EXPERIENCE:** | Office trainer, *Home Savings & Loan*, Yourtown, 2014 to 2018:<br><br>Trained tellers to banking and money handling procedures. Provided teller services. |
| **EDUCATION:** | Business management, 60 hours, *Anystate University*. |

# Resume of Jerome Robert Mechanic

**554 Oak Lane   *   Anytown, Anystate 11111   *   (555) 555-5555   *   <u>jrmechanic@fiction.net</u>**

Versatile, personable, highly motivated and results-oriented experienced
**Air Conditioning / Refrigeration Mechanic**,
with an associate's degree in air conditioning and refrigeration, a proven self-starter who enjoys
the challenge of working out an assignment and carrying it through to completion,
a problem solver and systems diagnostician with broad knowledge and extensive hands-on knowledge
of his craft, and a dependable, responsible team worker with recognized leadership qualities
seeks to put his knowhow to work for a quality, forward moving firm.

-=-=-=-=-=-=-=-=-=-=-=-=-=-=-=-=-=-=-=-=-=-=-=-=-=-=-=-=-=-=-=-=-=-=-=-=-=-=-=-=-=-=-=-=-=-=-=-

| | |
|---|---|
| HANDS-ON KNOWLEDGE OF: | All aspects of air conditioning and refrigeration maintenance.<br>High pressure boilers.<br>Programmable controllers.<br>Quality assurance procedures.<br>Computer programs, including QA and inventory control. |
| REFRIGERATION & AIR CONDITIONING MECHANICS EXPERIENCE: | *Anytown Food Processing, Inc.,* 2008 to present:<br>Refrigeration mechanic, November 2009 to present:<br><br>Responsible for maintenance of main ammonia refrigeration system, high pressure boilers and other heating and cooling systems of a food processing firm. Monitor and make operational adjustments to assure proper safe systems operation. Perform routine maintenance and repairs as needed. Perform quality control checks and inspections to assure compliance with company and governmental quality standards. Maintain appropriate Records of inspections and actions taken. |
| TEAM COORDINATION EXPERIENCE: | Team coordinator, *Anytown Food Processing, Inc.*, August 2012 to present:<br><br>Perform all duties, as above. In addition, working with a team of 6 key employees, participate in planning and developing a system for coordinating all production components for most efficient operation and most effective quality assurance.<br>Lead emergency response team.<br>Train new employees in QA procedures.<br>Maintain inventory control. |
| EDUCATION: | Associate degree, air conditioning & refrigeration, *Anytown Community College*<br>Currently enrolled, electrical & mechanical robotics, *Anytown C. C.* |

# Resume of George F. Productive

550 Maple Avenue   *   Anytown, Anystate 11111   *   (555) 555-5555

Versatile, personable, energetic, highly motivated and physically fit experienced
**ALL-ROUND PRODUCTION WORKER**,
a quick study who invariably performs above standards and stays with the job until it is done,
an industrious self-starter capable of carrying out broad responsibilities,
and a safety conscious trained firefighter, seeks a challenging position with a forward-
moving firm. Responsibilities may include forklift and /or equipment operations,
materials handling and supervision.

---

**HANDS-ON KNOWLEDGE OF:**

Inventory control/ materials handling.
Operation of forklift, portable air sanders, stamping press.
Operation of hydraulic equipment.
Safety procedures.
Firefighting techniques and procedures.
Emergency medical treatment.

**PRODUCTION EXPERIENCE:**

Forklift operator/production worker, *Yourtown Widget Co.*
September 2012 to present;

Operate forklift to prepare 6 to 7 truckloads of shipments per night. Filled in load sheets.
Operate stamping press and air sander. Consistently perform over 100% of quota to earn incentive bonuses.
Serve as member of fire brigade.

Tool crib attendant, October 2004 to 2006:

Provided tools and parts as needed for production. Assisted in determining needed parts to meet specifications.
Reorganized tool crib and installed inventory system for increase efficiency and ready availability.
Special assignment, June 2006: Inventoried tool crib to prepare for computerization. Developed computer input list.

Shipping/receiving supervisor, October 2007 to June 2014:

Directed the activities of one other person in loading and unloading trucks and arranging for shipment. Reported unit activities to traffic manager. Prepared bills of receiving and filed appropriate reports.

Custodian, *Anytown Board of Education*, September 2017 to September 2019:

Responsible for maintaining school buildings and grounds.

**EDUCATION:**

Secondary education, *Anystate University,* 2 years
Various firefighting and emergency medical treatment courses.

# Resume of Kathleen A. Worker

23 Elm Street   *   Anytown, Anystate 11111   *   (555) 555-5555

Versatile, adaptable, personable, reliable and conscientious experienced
**Allround Utility Worker / Supervisor,**
a proven performer with a broad variety of work experience who makes a point of making herself useful beyond the job description, an ambitious self-motivated quick study who enjoys a challenge, and a dependable results-producing problem solver who prides herself in accurate well-organized work, seeks to put her skills to work for a quality forward-moving firm.

O-o-o-o-o-o-o-o-o-o-o-o-o-o-o-o-o-o-o-o-o-o-o-o-o-o-o-o-o-o-o-o-o-o-o-o-o-o-o-o-o-o-o-o-o-o-o-o-O

| | |
|---|---|
| HANDS ON KNOWLEDGE OF: | Assembly of parts, operation of spot welding equipment.<br>Computer data entry.<br>Bookkeeping. Operation of a 10-key calculator<br>Money handling, including cash register operation and balancing receipts.<br>Customer contact: collection strategies and negotiation.<br>Payroll records and preparation.<br>Supervision, direction and motivation of employees. |
| SUPERVISORY EXPERIENCE: | *Allround Department store*, Anytown, February 2011 to April 2016:<br>Snack bar department head, March 2014 to April 2016:<br>Directed the activities of 3 employees in preparing and providing snack foods in an in-store facility. Oversaw cooking and cleaning. Trained workers. Took weekly inventory to determine needs. Ordered supplies. Received, unloaded and stored incoming supplies.<br>Operated cash register. Took in snack receipts.<br><br>Assistant head cashier, February 2012 to March 2014:<br>Provided services to support cashiers and insure smooth operations or cash registers. Made change of cashiers as required. Scheduled break times. Called cashiers from floor to reduce customer waiting.<br>At end of shift, inputted computer codes to determine daily total and balanced cash drawer. |
| ASSEMBLY EXPERIENCE: | Assembly worker, *Yourtown Widgets, Inc.,* August 2009 to January 2011:<br>Assembled 1000 thermostats per day from parts. Operated spot welding Equipment to attach 5000 contacts per day to parts. |
| BOOKKEEPING EXPERIENCE: | Bookkeeper, *Rapidvan Trucking Company,* May 2010 to present (part time) |
| EDUCATION: | Graduate, *Anytown High School*, small business management curriculum |

# John N. Process

125 Washington Street    Anytown, Anystate 11111
(555) 123-4567    <u>jnprocess@fiction.net</u>

Susan Q. Bigboss, Personnel Director
Bigmajor Company
PO Box 000
Bigcity, Yourstate 22222

Dear Ms. Bigboss:

    I recently learned of the opening you have in your enterprise. I believe that my extensive background as a Process Engineer and Manager will enable me to make significant contributions to improve your process design, making it more efficient and effective.

    I have been principal engineer for a major automotive rubber injection molding supplier for some years, I have comprehensive knowledge of the properties of rubber and rubber molding injection equipment. I am currently responsible for 25 presses.

    I have strong analytic capability. I am able to diagnose problems and visualize solutions in three dimensions. I have collaborated with another engineer in enhancing a design to obtain a patent which created a $4 million exclusive market for my present firm. My goal is to help the firm I work for build and maintain a strong profit position.

    As a manager, I know how to gain the respect of employees under my direction, how to inspire them and to motivate them into turning in superior performances. I know how to build a team approach. Using these skills for a former employer, I was able to turn a money-losing operation into a profit-making business within two years of assuming direction.

    My resume is enclosed along with a letter of recommendation.

    I'd like to meet with you soon in order to discuss what I can contribute to the profitability of your operations. Please contact me at the above address, phone or email so we can set a date for our meeting.

    My family and I are excited about the possibility of relocating to your area and I am looking forward to meeting you and exploring our mutual possibilities.

    Sincerely,

    John N. Process

Enclosures

# Russell R. Reliable
**225 Main Street, Anytown, Anystate 11111**
**555 555-5555**


Box 161, Anytown Gazette
333 Madison Avenue
Anytown, Anystate 11111

Dear Sirs:

I was very pleased to see your recent ad in the Anytown Gazette for a facilities engineering manager. The position you describe seems to match my background and experience exactly! I'd like to meet you to discuss just how I can contribute toward making your operations even more efficient and effective.

For the past eleven years as project manager for a chemical products manufacturing firm, I've worked extensively in designing and redesigning electrical, mechanical and hydraulic components of manufacturing equipment. I've also designed liquid waste management systems to meet EPA standards as well as building layouts. I am familiar with state-of-the-art technology in these areas.

Earlier, I was maintenance foreman for a large home appliance manufacturer with some 40 skilled tradespeople under my direction. I understand all aspects of maintenance management.

I've provided details of both these positions and my educational background in the enclosed resume.

I'm excited about the possibilities of working with your management team to get results for you. I'd like to meet with you soon to talk about how I can contribute to your enterprise. Please contact me at the above address to set up the date and time.

I am looking forward to meeting you and to working together to bring success to your business.

Very cordially yours,

Resume enclosed                                                              Russell R. Reliable

# Thomas A. Technician

333 Maple Avenue   *   Anytown, Anystate 11111
(555) 987-1234   *   thomtech@fiction.com

ABCD Corporation
2222 Market Street
Bigtown, Anystate 22222
Attn: RST Personnel Dept.

I saw your ad for an electronics technician in the *Bigtown Post*. I believe my experience and training enable me to meet your requirements and make a positive contribution to servicing such electronic devices as vending machines and other equipment.

As you can see from the enclosed resume, I've just graduated with an associate degree in electronics from *Anytown Community College*. While there, I maintained a 3.8 GPA.

I have other knowledge that could prove useful to your field service operations. I am an experienced welder and cutter, having gotten this training and experience with the U.S. Army.

I know how to work with and persuade people. I've worked as a telemarketer making cold calls.

More recently, I've been working as a bartender and developing the skills needed to deal effectively and tactfully with even difficult people.

I am flexible, willing to take on a variety of assignments to get the kind of job done that will help ABCD hold onto its current clients because they're happy about the service and help bring in new clients because of your fine service reputation.

I am willing to relocate and travel as the job requires. I will be happy to undergo training to your requirements and your equipment if that is needed.

I'd like to meet with you to discuss how I can contribute to making ABCD's field service one of the best in the country. You can reach me to set up an appointment at the above address or you can call me at work at (555) 987-4334.

I'd be proud to be associated with your firm. I'm looking forward to meeting with you and talking with you about your plans for your field service team and how I might fit into those plans. I hope we can do that in the near future.

Very sincerely yours,

Thomas A. Technician

Resume enclosed

**Joanne W. Thorough**
822 Oak Place, Anytown, Anystate 11111
555 987-4321
jwthorough@fiction.com


John H. Bigboss, President
Major Hotels, Inc.
P.O. Box 123
Yourtown, Yourstate 22222

Your organization came to my attention as a forward-moving quality operation. I would be proud to be associated with you as a member of your management team. I believe that my extensive track record of achievement in management will enable me to make many positive contributions toward moving your enterprise forward.

You'll see from my enclosed resume I have some twelve years experience as manager of two full service quality hotels. Under my leadership, one of them was consistently ranked among the top ten of a 660-hotel chain.

Working well with people is my specialty. I know how to motivate employees to high productivity by encouraging a team spirit, I know how to deal with the public and with representatives of large corporations to ensure their satisfaction.

I thrive on handling a variety of management tasks at the same time. I strongly believe in the work ethic, in putting in full effort to get the job done and done well. I know how to develop a budget and how to keep to it.

I'd very much like to meet with you to discuss what I can contribute toward making your operations even more successful. I will contact you to set up an appointment for a discussion. Alternatively, you can reach me at the above address, phone or email address.

I am looking forward to meeting you and hope that we can come to a mutually profitable arrangement.

Yours for effective management

Resume enclosed                                                       Joanne W. Thorough

# Maria Market
### 789 Beach Drive * Holiday Lakes
### Anytown, Anystate 11111
### (555) 567-7890  *  <u>mariamarket@fiction.net</u>

John Q. Saleschief, Sales Manager
Independent Outside Sales, Inc.
222 Enterprise Road
Yourtown, Anystate, 11112

Dear Mr. Saleschief:

    Our mutual friend, Chester Knowemall, suggested that I contact you about the opening in your sales staff you told him about. Thank you for taking the time to review my qualifications. I believe that my extensive experience and proven track record in sales will fulfill the requirements of that opening. I'm looking forward to working with you as a member of your sales team. My resume is enclosed.

    My most recent position enabled me to build up a network of quality contacts for the sale of industrial equipment throughout the country. I have spoken with and worked with people on all levels from company presidents to shipping clerks. I appreciate their requirements and viewpoints.

    I have a natural talent for sales. I know how to find solutions to client problems with appropriate products. I enjoy the challenge of taking on difficult sales assignments. I know how to negotiate and how to close a sale.

    I enjoy using my skills to help a company succeed. I'm extraordinarily creative. I've developed logos and sales slogans for several small businesses. I look for creative solutions to generate business.

    I'd like to get together with you to discuss your firm's goals and how I can contribute to reaching them. I'm excited about what I've learned from Chester, another mutual friend, Pat Salesstar, and others and want to learn more. I can be reached at the above address, telephone or email address. Let's set up an appointment so that I can show you what I can do.

    I'm looking forward to meeting with you. I hope we can do business together.

                                                    Sincerely yours,

                                                  Maria Market

Resume enclosed

**Constance C. Constant**
**135 South Oak Street**
**Anytown, Anystate 11111**
**(555) 654-3579**

Jerry Doitall, Manager
Yourtown Widgets, Inc.
453 Market Street
Yourtown, Anystate 11112

Dear Mr. Doitall:

My attention was attracted to your company by your fine reputation as a quality operation. I'd like to put my engineering management skills to work for you to help you boost productivity and innovation while cutting costs to the bone. I've gotten quite good at this in my recent supervisory positions.

I also hold a master's degree in mechanical engineering from Anystate University.

My personal philosophy of management includes being completely loyal to the organization while acting as a team leader to set objectives, formulate strategies and plan for their efficient execution. I believe in setting an example of contagious enthusiasm, in providing positive guidance and in maintaining a teamwork environment for achieving mutual goals.

I am dedicated to helping employees find personal job satisfaction and growth as they solve complex engineering problems, to experience challenge, responsibility and participation so that they can turn in maximum performance.

I look at problems as opportunities to come up with creative solutions. I see conflict as an opportunity to bring people with a common interest together. I am skilled at identifying and resolving problems most beneficially for everyone concerned.

I have a track record of putting together efficient cost-effective organizations and setting records for accomplishment.

I'd be proud to be associated with your firm because I know that you are interested in including an enthusiastic, energetic, honest and self-motivated woman who is a proven performer in your management team.

I'd like to get together with you to discuss how my knowledge, engineering knowhow and management experience can help you make your organization more effective. As you can see from the enclosed resume, I have performed well in three different management areas.

I can be reached at the above address and telephone or, during working hours, at (555) 234-5434. I am looking forward to meeting you and how we will have a long, long mutually profitable association.

Yours very truly,


Constance Constant                                                                                     Resume enclosed

# SECTION D

## CARRYING OUT YOUR JOB SEARCH

# ORGANIZING YOUR JOB SEARCH: WHERE TO LOOK

Where do employers go when looking to fill a job opening in your field? That's precisely ***where you want to be*** as a job hunter so they can find you! The most successful job-search strategies are built around finding answers to that question and proceeding accordingly.

Answers vary somewhat with the type of job opening to be filled and the nature of the business enterprise. Employers use different strategies for locating high-level managers and highly specialized professionals than for production workers or minimally skilled workers for minimum wages.

Nevertheless, most employers follow similar procedures for seeking help. Knowing what they are will help you design your effective job-search strategy.

Keep in mind that, just like you, every employer with a job opening has a serious problem: For optimum results for his business, he must find a ***reliable*** someone to carry out a specific task or series of tasks. Not having those tasks performed reliably could result in dire consequences for his business.

His emphasis is on that word, "reliable!" It's not just that the tasks have to be performed reliably. He needs someone who will stick around as long as needed so that in a few months or years he won't be faced with the very same serious problem once again, perhaps with the serious tasks uncompleted.

Just like the typical job seeker, the typical employer with a job opening is staring out into the great unknown. He knows that reliable someone is out there somewhere and may even be seeking his very job. How can he locate her when he has no idea just who or where she is?

## *Working your network*

With that word, *"reliable,"* in mind, the typical employer is happiest when dealing with quantities known to him. So, at least for certain types of jobs, such as management, office, production and sales staff, he's likely to start his search among people he knows. That way, he has the word of someone he trusts that a candidate is reliable.

Whom does he know? If he does not already have someone in mind, usually he starts by talking about the opening with management within his own company, golfing buddies and other close personal friends, colleagues doing similar work (if that doesn't reveal company secrets to them), his family and members of his service clubs or the local Chamber of Commerce.

If he knows of someone working for a competitor with a good track record and the right qualifications, he may contact her directly or indirectly through a go-between.

Next, he posts the position for his current employees. There may be talent among his own workers that he wasn't previously aware of. Current employees, having already demonstrated their reliability, may be looking to move up the career ladder a rung or two. Current employees have family and friends with the right qualifications who are job-hunting.

Current employees are expected to have some understanding of the needs of the firm they work for. They may even have some understanding of the requirements of the job to be filled and the type of person needed to fill the job.

Recommendations of current reliable employees are widely regarded as the best source of reliable new employees. So, up goes the job notice onto the firm's bulletin board, into a memo to employees and into the company newsletter.

> ### *HIGH IMPACT TIP*
> For the reasons cited above, the very best place to begin your effective job search is by spreading the word that you are job-hunting among your personal network of family, friends, professional associates, colleagues and even present and former co-workers. Talk about your job search with other members at meetings of your clubs, community service clubs, professional associations, your church and any other place you can think of!
>
> It's very possible that your network interconnects with the network of an employer with the right job to be filled. It's even possible that you are talking with your next employer.

> ### *HIGH IMPACT TIP*
> Be sure to check the bulletin board where job openings are posted in your current place of employment, particularly if you're looking to advance your career and like your employer. Your ideal job may be waiting for you there.
>
> Job posting bulletin boards are also maintained in many schools, public and school libraries and your state employment agency office.

# Headhunters

Many employers, especially the larger ones, next turn to an employment agency (often referred to as "headhunters"), especially for professional and management job openings or for those highly specialized fields where talent is scarce. Many agencies specialize in placing candidates in a specific field or closely-related fields, such as health care specialties or engineering and other scientific specialties.

An agency may even already have lists of possible candidates in hand. These are provided by headhunters as a courtesy and a way of drumming up business for the agency by developing openings for their job seekers.

Indeed, an ongoing relationship is almost always in place between more competent agencies and those most likely to be involved in the hiring process within many large corporations. Professional recruiters spend much of their time assiduously cultivating such relations so that they themselves remain solvent.

The role of a headhunter is to find a match between employer requirements and a job seeker's qualifications and then to put the two in contact with each other.

Most usually, she does this by first screening resumes to ensure that there is the possibility of a match between the job seeker's qualifications and the employer's requirements. She then provides the job seeker's resume to the prospective employer for review. When interest is shown, she gives the job seeker the name and contact information of the employer so that an interview can be scheduled.

For this service, she or her agency collects a healthy fee. For most of the jobs she handles, the fee is paid by the employer. For other jobs where the supply of available workers is plentiful, the job seeker is expected to pay the fee, Many headhunting firms recruit only for employer-paid positions.

### *HIGH IMPACT TIP*

As a rule of thumb, if the job you're seeking requires paying a recruiting fee, you can probably find a job more readily some other way. A great many such jobs are never referred to headhunters. Moreover, the fee can be a substantial part of your first year's salary. Under these circumstances, use an employment agency only as a last resort.

Especially for those in whose profession the expectation is that they will relocate for their next job, using the services of a professional recruiter makes a lot of sense. Many headhunting firms are national or even international in scope and can present you with a much wider array of possibilities than you will find through other means.

# Professional conventions and job fairs

For many specialized professional jobs, one of the better sources of reliable employees is the national or regional convention of that field's professional association. Many of the top performers in that field can be expected to attend its convention.

Professional conventions are usually held in large hotels. Large firms often maintain hospitality suites during conventions with a dual purpose of selling their products and attracting potential key employees.

A job seeker with appropriate qualifications can find in such a meeting a superior source of quality job leads in your field. They provide an excellent way to establish personal contact with employers or their representatives who may provide an on-the-spot interview.

Often sponsored by a local educational institution or even the local media, job fairs are used by employers in your area to find quality employees. The job seeker who shows the initiative to attend a job fair may well turn out to be a high quality reliable employee.

Job fairs provide opportunities for direct communication with employers or their representatives. An appointment for an interview can sometimes be made directly on the spot. More often, your resume is left with the possibility of the employer contacting you.

Job fairs are most appropriate for those seeking less specialized positions, especially those positions most in demand by a variety of employers, such as accounting, sales and production work.

When sponsored by an educational institution for its recent or upcoming graduates, job fairs can also be a means for finding specialized positions. This is particularly true of educational institutions specializing in training for a specific field or group of fields.

# Advertising

Employers often use advertising as a method of last resort for finding quality employees. Other methods discussed above are much more cost-effective and likely to yield reliable results.

For the employer, the cost of advertising a position is much more than the price of the ad. The process of screening responses, especially if the response is heavy, is labor-intensive. Responses must be screened. Many responses can be expected to be grossly inappropriate to the position to be filled. Also, when an ad is placed, there is no one to vouch directly for the reliability of information given by respondents. This must be determined by other means, also labor-intensive.

For this reason, a great many quality job openings are never advertised at all. Employers prefer the methods outlined above, over which they believe they have more control.

An important exception is administrative positions in government on any level. These usually are required by law to be openly advertised or publicized.

Whether and where an employer an employer places an ad varies with many factors:

- ➢ The nature of the business, its scope and geographic location influence whether the ad will be placed in local, regional or national or even international media.

- ➢ The size of the firm and its recruiting budget often dictate where ads will be placed. For national ads, funds must be available for relocating new incoming employees.

- ➢ The nature of jobs to be filled may decide where an ad is placed and whether it will be placed at all. When needed workers are available in plentiful supply, why use broader advertising? When positions require highly specialized expertise, an employer may need to cast a wider net.

- ➢ The number of jobs to be filled may decide whether an ad is placed at all. Where much new staffing is anticipated, as in the startup of a new firm or new project for an existing business, an ad campaign is more likely to be conducted. When only a few jobs need to be filled, the employer is very likely to rely on other methods described previously, resorting to advertising only as a last ditch effort.

- ➢ Economic cycles also play their role. When unemployment is low and workers are scarce, employers use different tactics than when the reverse is true.

- ➢ An employer's previous experience with advertising in various media also comes into play. Like the rest of us, he is more likely to repeat successful experiences of the past.

## National Media

Sunday editions of very large metropolitan dailies, such as *The New York Times* or *The Los Angeles Times* and several others are the prime national media for job placement. This would include their Internet editions. They are popular with large firms advertising to fill specialized professional and higher or middle management positions. Usually, such ads have a relatively quick turnaround time in producing results for the employer.

## Specialized Professional Publications

For professional jobs that require specialized expertise the usual ads may produce few responses. An employer may then advertise such positions in relevant trade and professional publications that such an expert is likely to read. Depending on publication schedules, he must take into account a time delay between placement of an ad and expected responses.

## The Internet

Internet technology is still so new and rapidly developing that anything said in these pages may well be obsolete by the time of publication.

Nevertheless, more and more employers are discovering the Internet a rapidly growing, relatively inexpensive and highly effective medium for locating specific desirable high-tech-oriented employees. At the same time, more and more sites dedicated to the job market are being developed. Many firms have websites and Facebook pages, or the like, on which job openings can be accessed. Also, headhunting firms and the various media maintain such websites and Facebook pages.

The principles discussed in these pages are equally applicable to seeking a job through the Internet.

## Regional Media

Smaller and medium-sized firms with smaller recruiting budgets or more limited needs are likely to turn to regional advertising. Not only is the cost of advertising less than for a national campaign, relocation costs are also likely to be smaller. Indeed, there may be no need at all for new employees to relocate at the employer's expense.

To recruit specialized professional and middle management positions, this usually means placing an ad in the Sunday edition of a large metropolitan daily with a broad regional readership, including their Internet editions.

## Local Media

Local media, including small metropolitan dailies and weekday ads in a large metropolitan and even national newspapers with their Internet editions usually are for clerical, service and production jobs. Because there is a sufficient supply of local people qualified for these jobs and no cost benefit, there is no perceived need to advertise them more broadly.

# ORGANIZING YOUR JOB SEARCH: HOW TO LOOK

For those who *TAKE CHARGE of their careers*, mapping out an effective job search is a whole lot like laying out an effective sales campaign. Basic strategies are similar:

➢ Likely potential employers are identified as qualified as capable of providing an opportunity and appropriate setting for advancing your career.

➢ When possible, the specific person or members of the team within the qualified employer's firm who make hiring decisions for the position you seek are identified for contact.

➢ Contact is made with qualified prospective employers to set up an opportunity for discussion.

➢ Precise employer needs that match specific services you are able and willing to provide are identified and explored with the employer.

➢ Terms are negotiated to the satisfaction of both parties.

➢ Finally, once satisfactory terms have been reached, *you must make the sale!* That is, you must convince a qualified employer that your services meet her needs more effectively than those of competitors.

Approaching your job search as a sales campaign puts you in charge of the process by making you a proactive partner. By becoming proactive, you make for yourself significantly greater possibilities for ending up with a job you like with opportunities for career growth and development. At the same time, you put yourself in a position for making useful contributions to an enterprise you have confidence in.

## *Identifying and contacting potential employers*

You've already determined just what your qualifications are and just what position or range of positions you're aiming for. You did so by spending time and effort to go through the steps of preparing your *HIGH-IMPACT Resume* as outlined in **Section B**.

Those procedures and the resulting resume have given you a handle on the direction you want to take with your career while leaving the door wide open for other attractive opportunities. That knowledge, together with the resulting **HIGH-IMPACT Resume,** forms a solid starting point for your successful job search.

Where do you go from here? How do you get your **HIGH-IMPACT Resume** into the hands of a quality employer seeking to fill the position you have in mind?

In the previous chapter, the process followed by employers in locating reliable employees was outlined. Curiously, most typical job seekers conduct their search in reverse order. Many, if not almost all of them, begin – and end – their search by scouring the classified section of their local newspapers and answering those ads.

By limiting their job search in this fashion, they also limit their possibilities and probably their income. As noted in the preceding chapter, local classified ads are used primarily for jobs on the lower end of the pay scale, jobs without specialized qualifications.

Many, many excellent positions for which you may qualify offer you greater opportunities and are never advertised.

In contrast, emulating topnotch sales specialists, the **TAKE-CHARGE Career Manager** plans his job search in such a way that he can take or make every opportunity to get that special position that he wants: the job that will put his career on the fast track to where he wants to go and enable him to establish the lifestyle he wants. He plans it in such a fashion that he "just happens" to be where employers with a position to fill are looking and may even add an option for creating his own position.

---

### *HIGH-IMPACT TIP*

Throughout your job search, you'll get optimum results by staying positive, proactive and upbeat.

Leave any unfortunate experiences from your previous job behind you! This is not the time to talk about any raw deal you may have gotten or what is wrong with your previous place of employment. Allowing yourself to dwell on your misfortunes, even in the privacy of your mind, will not get you optimum results. What you say tends to reflect what you are thinking about.

Instead, direct your thinking and talk to your positive qualities. Concentrate your energies on the quality of your experience and know-how and where you want to take your career. This, more than anything else, will help you to *TAKE CHARGE of your Career!*

## *Work your network*

A great place to start your job search is working your personal network. Let friends and family know that you are seeking new work. Talk about your job search with those you meet in your various social activities and organizations! Where it does not jeopardize your current job, talk to colleagues as well! If you are in a specialized line of work, bring up your search in conversing with others in your profession.

The more people who are aware of your search, the more likely it is that one of them will connect you with your next employer. Their recommendations of you to an employer are worth their weight in gold! In essence, they are vouching for your reliability, any employer's prime concern.

Ask each person you discuss your search with to pass the word along, to check job postings where they work, to put in a word to their bosses about you and your qualifications and, where your experience matches job requirements, to pass your resume on to possible employers.

By working your network, you build your network. The existence of that network may give you an edge in your new job simply because you have a network to tap into for the benefit of your next employer, thereby increasing your value to your new firm.

## *Check job postings*

The job you're seeking may be available in your present place of employment. This has the advantage of allowing you to move up the career ladder while preserving your current seniority and benefits. Many companies post job openings as they become available. Given appropriate qualifications, current productive employees are actually preferred for these positions because they have demonstrated their reliability.

Jobs posted by educational institutions are most usually entry-level jobs. If you are in that market, it's an excellent place to look. Many companies use this means to attract new young talent.

A wide range of jobs on all levels is posted by your state employment agency. These include government jobs, which usually offer superior security, pay and benefits.

## *Attend conventions & job fairs*

For specialized professionals, your professional association's convention or conference offers golden opportunities for **HIGH-IMPACT Career Managers** to make useful connections.

At such meetings, you can extend your network, make new friends, and talk about your job search over lunch or at informal get-togethers with your counterparts from many other companies. Your newfound friends and old acquaintances may even agree to pass your resume to recruiters within their own companies.

As a matter of both sales and recruiting strategy, various large and medium-sized companies sponsor hospitality suites within or near hotels or convention centers where professional meetings are held. They do so expressly to provide opportunities for representatives of their recruiting staffs to connect with job-hunters like you.

Those who make a point of attending their profession's conferences are thought to be better performers on the job. They have the appearance at least of making a point of keeping up with their field. They have also provided themselves with a network of contacts within the field, a network which may benefit the firm that hires them.

Headhunting firms set up hospitality suites for the same purpose. Making the rounds of hospitality suites with resume in hand in order to set up connections could prove very productive in your job search.

Meetings of the area or state chapter of your professional association can also be made into an occasion to work your network. Once again, ask each friend to pass your resume and the friend's recommendation of you along to his employer and other companies that might hire you.

For those in less specialized lines of work, job fairs often prove very productive sources of useful job leads. Employers participate in job fairs with the specific intention to recruit staff with specific positions in mind. Recruiters are on hand to talk to you. The opportunities are too good to pass up.

### *HIGH-IMPACT TIP*

Carry a plentiful supply of resumes with you to pass on at conferences, meetings and job fairs. These should already be folded and placed in envelopes beforehand so that you can simply hand it to contacts when the occasion arises. Copies of a letter of recommendation can be placed in the same envelope. The envelope both presents a more professional appearance, suggesting that you are a class act, and protects the resumes from casual mishandling.

## Working through headhunters

Names of professional recruiting firms in your area can be found in employment ads in the classified sections of large metropolitan dailies, the yellow pages of large metropolitan phone books, or by googling them on the Internet. As noted above, professional recruiters also work professional conferences and job fairs. A friend or colleague who has had a positive experience with a headhunter may make a recommendation of an effective recruiter who is likely to get results for you.

Some agencies serve more local areas and may give you more personal service for that reason. Such agencies often place a wider variety of positions than national or regional agencies by including clerical and factory jobs. Their names ae usually found in your local classifieds or phone book.

For those seeking specialized professional and higher management positions, assistance of a professional recruiter is invaluable. He can place your resume in the hands of many employers you might not otherwise consider, including those at some geographic remove from your current locality.

Most recruiters do business mainly by phone. To obtain their services simply phone them or visit their website. When word gets out about your availability for job placement, they may also contact you by phone.

The recruiter will have a brief conversation with you to determine what kind of work you are seeking. If in the area, he may ask to interview you in person. In any case, he will ask for your resume and send copies to his client companies.

> ## *HIGH-IMPACT TIP*
> 
> In dealing with an employment agency, it is wise to keep in mind that the person you are talking to is effectively working for employers who use her services. They pay her fees. They are her repeat customers whose business she wants to keep. You, your skills and experience are the product she's selling. Therefore, an individual job searcher is much more expendable to a headhunter than is an employer.
>
> Categorically, do not say anything to a headhunter that you wouldn't say to a prospective employer! Most especially, say nothing derogatory about any former employer and discuss none of the unfortunate circumstances that may have led to your job search!
>
> The foregoing point cannot be emphasized enough! Many a job seeker has disqualified himself from being hired or being represented by employment agencies by complaining about former employers. Find another shoulder to cry on!
>
> Be positive and upbeat. Otherwise, you'll be waiting a long time for action and your resume may never make it to an employer's desk.

> **HIGH-IMPACT TIP**
>
> It may prove productive to place your name with two to four headhunting firms. While most will not tell you precisely which companies they serve, except for those they specifically have in mind for you, they usually will discuss the nature of businesses they specialize in serving, if any, the range of company sizes and geographic area they serve. For broad coverage, select agencies serving differing constituencies consistent with the line of work you are seeking.
>
> Limit the number of agencies you use. Employers receiving the very same resume from several agencies at the same time tend to think "desperate job seeker!"
>
> Similarly, when a headhunter calls to place you with more than one employer and hears, "We've already talked to him. He was referred by another agency," she is likely to stop making efforts on your behalf.

## Answering ads

Answering ads found in any media, including the Internet, is very similar to taking a shot in the dark. Your main challenge is to make your response stand out so distinctly from all other responses that it engages the interest of the resume reviewer who collects them. Your **HIGH-IMPACT Resume** is designed to do just that!

Follow any directions in the ad explicitly. Make sure that you include all information asked for, with the single exception of precise salary requirements. Many responses are disqualified for the simple reason that they didn't provide information asked for or follow directions.

> ## HIGH-IMPACT TIP
> ***Do not include salary requirements when answering ads!*** Doing so puts you in a lose/lose double bind. Stating salary requirements before your interview with the employer is very likely to cause you problems later. It boxes you in when negotiating for a salary.
>
> The problem is that stating your exact salary requirements gives resume reviewers a reason to disqualify you without an interview. Should your stated figure be higher than the employer anticipates or is budgeted for, he won't call you for an interview. If it is lower than he thinks it ought to be for that job, he will write you off as a probable poor performer or someone with personality problems and also won't interview you.
>
> Women, particularly, should be wary about complying with such a request. Your response may keep you out of a career track matching your potential.
>
> An appropriate response to a request for salary requirements before an interview is that you'll discuss them during negotiations.

In answering ads, take advantage of the golden opportunity to present your qualifications in two complementary ways by including a cover letter written for the occasion with your resume. This gives resume reviewers two pieces of paper to read about you, while underlining and expanding on your qualifications and making a positive impression on employers.

Base the text of each cover letter on the text of the particular ad and whatever pertinent data you find out about the company. When specific skills or experience are cited in the ad, be sure to stress how your skills and experience match the requirements. If the name of the company is mentioned, state your high regard for that firm and your desire to be part of its team.

Your local public library has many resources of information about various firms. Your librarian will assist you in locating it. The Internet is another source of information. Research may provide clues to how you can help the company to succeed. Talking about this is the theme of your cover letter.

Many employers place blind ads. These do not identify the employer. Responses are sent to a box number at the newspaper to further protect the employer's identity. Such ads are even more challenging to answer because you have no resources of information beyond the ad. You must rely on the text of the ad and educated guesses about the nature of the job and employer to write your cover letter.

Where too little information is given, you are well-advised to focus your job search elsewhere.

There is also the possibility that you may be responding to your current employer. Use your best judgment about whether this will affect you positively or negatively.

# *Creating your own job and other over-the-transom approaches*

It takes daring, imagination, foresight and chutzpah to create your own job. Looking for that ideal job that fits your skills, experience and plans for advancing your career, you've found nothing that fits your requirements in the job market. You may have a brilliant idea about a service that no one else has ever thought of. Alternately, you've become aware of a service new to your locality. So, you set out to define a job for yourself.

Keeping an eye out to make an opportunity, you see a need for an in-house service, usually in a specific industry or for a specific firm. The employer you target may not be aware of her need for service in this area. Since you have appropriate skills and experience to solve a problem for her by providing it, your next task is to convince her that she needs it and that you are just the best person to provide it for her.

Your first step is to study all aspects of the need you've discerned thoroughly so you can design a job description around it. What are the functions of this job? What tasks will you perform in a single day or week? Using this information, you can follow the steps of SECTION A of this book to draw up a **HIGH-IMPACT Resume** directed toward the job you hope to fill.

For a dream job that doesn't fall into the usual categories of work with which the employer may be familiar, yet another possibility is to draw up a one-page brochure or proposal to accompany your resume and cover letter. This spells out the advantages of the service you are proposing. How does it impact employer finances, time, efficiency or any other aspect of her business in a positive way?

An ***over-the-transom*** approach to possible employers is yet another possibility to be used whenever you find little demand for your specific skills after a thorough search of the usual channels to employment discussed earlier in this chapter. It's also useful when defining an entirely new job. In this approach, you go directly to an employer who has neither placed an ad nor otherwise made her need for filling such a job known.

With your **HIGH-IMPACT Resume**, coupled with a proposal or brochure, and a sound grasp of the work you are seeking in hand, the next step is to identify and qualify possible employers.

You may have a specific firm or industry to approach with your proposal already in mind, possibly even your present employer. Whether you do or not, there are many sources of the data you need: Your local library, the Internet, news reports, your personal network, your trade or professional association, the Chamber of Commerce in the community in which the firm is located and current or former employees of the firm are some examples of information sources.

Taking the identification process one step further, you next determine the precise management or professional person within your targeted firm who will most benefit from your proposed service and the person will make the decision about hiring you if that is a different person. These are the people to whom you will direct your campaign.

Start with the person you infer will most benefit from your service. With her backing, your proposal has greater chances for success. If thoroughly convinced, she may help you present it to the decision-maker. If she is not convinced, consider whether to proceed with this firm very carefully. Her serious opposition could work against you long after you have landed the job. Best take your proposal elsewhere.

For many positions, especially less specialized jobs with many possible target firms, contact can be made by mail, or email. Send your resume package to contacts within the firm.

A more proactive method, especially useful for high management and specialized professional positions, is to approach your contact directly. Set up a face-to-face meeting or take her to dinner. This can be done directly if you are acquainted with the contact, or indirectly through your network. Especially proactive job seekers can make the opportunity for contact through making sure that they are where the contact is likely to be when she is likely to be there and striking up a friendship.

# QUALIFYING EMPLOYERS

The typical job seeker takes just about any job that happens to be offered to him after the shortest job search possible. He focuses solely on personal risk-free safety and job security. If offered two or three jobs, he chooses the one that seems to offer the best pay and benefits as his main and probably his only criterion.

His concerns center on what the employer expects from him and how well he thinks he can meet those expectations. He's never taken time or cared enough to consider explicitly what his own expectations and needs might be or how a prospective employer might meet them. Rather, he expects employers to know and provide what he wants from a job by somehow reading his mind.

Consequently, as often as not in his new job, he finds himself as dissatisfied, unproductive and unhappy as he was in earlier jobs. He repeatedly winds up in an uncomfortable, unfriendly work environment conducive to neither career nor personal growth. Only after he accepts the job and begins working does he realize what he has gotten into and begins to complain loudly or to sulk. Instead of realizing a career, he merely counts down the time to retirement.

As his on-the-job troubles mount, he grows more and more cynical and disillusioned with work in general and his career and his current employer in particular. With that, his productivity stagnates or drops significantly. If that doesn't trigger an early release from his job, it shunts him onto a low career track.

If driven to total desperation, he may initiate a job-hunting cycle yet another time. However, he's far more likely to hang on to any job he has for dear life because, after all, it *is* a job and there *is* a paycheck coming in.

In contrast, a **TAKE CHARGE Career Manager** is a whole lot choosier about job offers she's willing to consider, even about potential employers she interviews. She fully realizes that ensuring proper settings and conditions for her career and job satisfaction is as much her responsibility as that of the firm she works for.

"*Qualifying*" is a concept borrowed from sales strategy. Before approaching a potential sale, a proficient sales specialist **qualifies** the customer both to determine the customer's needs that can be met by the sale and to ensure a match between buyer and product or service.

The **TAKE-CHARGE Career Manager** finds job hunting a challenge. It's her opportunity to look around, to find out what's happening in the real world beyond the sheltered work environment she's been in up to now. It's an opportunity to consider a range of possibilities and evaluate her career progress. What she observes and hears from the people she meets during the hunt may provide information about possibilities that comes to her more easily and directly than any other way.

**Qualifying** an employer begins well before the first contact. It progresses through all the interviews right up to acceptance of a job.

**Qualifying** an employer means checking out a prospective employer to ensure that the company is a viable place to work. In this process, you check out the nature of the assignment, the work environment, comfort level and opportunities for advancement provided, as well as pay and benefits, to determine if and how well they meet your requirements and expectations.

Coincidentally, information gained in the process of qualifying an employer is likely to prove very useful during your interview and subsequent salary negotiations. It provides topics for discussion and a basis for decisions. It suggests aspects of your experience and qualifications you should emphasize in order to maximize results. The very fact that you have even done this research makes a powerful impression on potential employers. Researching a business just doesn't usually occur to typical job seekers.

**Qualifying** employers is conducted in much the same way that employers use to qualify potential employees. A process of elimination empowers you to make your choice from the best options available to you.

Our main thesis of the *TAKE-CHARGE Approach to Career Management* is that job-hunting is a two-way street! It's not just about figuring out and trying to conform to what employers are looking for. It's not about putting up a front so that they will talk to you.

It's about *your* potential job satisfaction as much as it's about meeting your next employer's expectations. It's about finding, creating and achieving the job *you* are after too. It's about meeting and melding *your* concerns and expectations with those of the employer you choose. It's about setting up a proactive relationship with an employer. It's about interacting proactively in partnership with an employer to meet mutual objectives.

Your career choice is one of the few really important life decisions you will ever make. It ranks right up there with your choice of a spouse in determining the course of your life.

We identify ourselves and other people almost entirely by our occupations. Right after learning someone's name, we ask what he does for a living.

Every occupation creates its own role for those who follow it and partly defines who we are. We think of ourselves as engineer or manager or carpenter or secretary. We are expected to think and act in a certain way because of the kind of work we do. We devote years to learning specific roles associated with our occupations and become permeated with their world outlook and mystique.

Your choice of the environment in which to carry out your occupation ranks just behind your choice of the career itself in determining the course of your life. You spend a significant part of your life in your workplace carrying out your work goals, sometimes more than you do in sleeping or interacting with your family or friends. Often, the people you meet on the job make up your main circle of friends.

Company practices and policies along with the attitudes and ideas of those you work with both as colleagues and clients play a major role in forming your ideas and worldview.

All of this underlines making the right choices for the best fit available as a desired outcome of your job search. Your happiness and your future are at stake!

**Qualifying** an employer is the means whereby you set up an optimally productive relationship with your next employer. You are able to do this because you have some idea of what he's like and what he is looking for before you talk to him. Taking these steps now can help ensure your job satisfaction and productivity down the road.

"Different strokes for different folks!" People vary so radically in personality, interests and desires. Some folks thrive on stress, finding that it stimulates their productivity. Others do okay with moderate stress but find that too high a level interferes with and even destroys their productivity. Still others require an almost stress free environment to function at all.

Some folk see in a failing company a sure route down the tubes to disaster. Others see the same operation as a challenge to provide leadership to turn the firm around or to take it in a different direction.

These differences make it unproductive to create a one-size-fits-all set of specifications for the precise factors that define the ideal work environment for you. You'll have to develop your own set of criteria for yourself. That's part and parcel of ***TAKING CHARGE of your career!***

What follows are brief descriptions of the kinds of information about an employer that you may want to check out before you make that life-impacting decision of accepting a job in the areas of stability of the business and workplace environment. Other factors may be important to you. In that case, you can add to the list of what you want to check out where appropriate. The weight to be placed on each factor is contingent on your specifications and expectations.

As stated previously, good sources of the data you need include the resource department of your local library, the Internet, news reports, your personal network, your professional or trade association and its publications, the Chamber of Commerce in the community in which the firm is located, and current or former employees of the firm.

## Stability of the business

Unless you're in the business of turning around failing business enterprises, you're likely to want to work for a stable, financially solvent business that's likely to be around at least until you're ready to move on. This makes it wise to look at the firm's business picture very early in the game, even before you agree to an interview.

Sources of this information are abundant. In addition to those listed above, check financial publications and stock market analyses. The Internet is a good source for these.

What do you want to know? Sample questions might be:

> Is the enterprise turning a profit? Consistent failure to turn a sufficient profit translates into failure to stay in business.

> Have there been recent management changes? How often have they occurred in recent years? Frequent management changes suggest instability.

> What's the status of the contract under which you will be working? Is one or more other contracts in the offing? Many large companies are contractors or subcontractors. The status of the contract indicates whether and how soon layoffs are likely.

> Precisely what are the nature of its products or services, especially in the subdivision you are considering.

Obviously, sudden unpredictable changes in business climate and sudden unforeseen reverses of an apparently stable firm's business fortunes are an historical reality. There are no guarantees against this happening even with extensive research.

At the same time, knowing whatever you can learn of the business outlook and financial situation you are going into potentially changes your odds of choosing lasting employment. Your research may possibly also help you make sound decisions in other such job-related areas as the degree of challenge this job will offer.

## *Workplace environment*

Information on some aspects of just what the environment you will work in is like, particularly whether it's worker-friendly to match your personal style, must often be obtained through indirect methods. Other aspects, such as the facilities provided, can be observed directly.

The environment you work in almost invariably has a strong bearing on the direction of your career. It can nurture you and help you grow. It can also put you on the defensive, set you back considerably and seriously impair your ability to produce. Only the strongest survive and thrive in a negative work environment.

Just like individual people, each place of business has its unique personality. Usually, but not entirely, its tone is determined by the personalities of its leadership, both companywide and locally. Personalities of individual staff members, interactions between them, interactions of staff with clients and vendors, company play and the nature of the business and its facilities all also play their role.

Your challenge is to find the environment which best suits *your* personal style. Again, environmental preferences vary markedly with personality. Some thrive in a highly structured environment where goals are set for them. Others feel that structure cramps productivity and prefer setting their own goals. Some excel under pressure of competition. Others prefer cooperation and mentoring to accomplish mutual goals.

Factors reflecting employer attitudes impact workplace environment include employee turnover rates, layoff history, facilities and company policies. These can be researched.

Employee turnover rates, especially for larger employers, can sometimes be determined in the early stages of research. A high turnover rate suggests unrealistic management expectations of employees, dissatisfied employees, overly intrusive management policies, or serious personality problems among those management levels interacting directly with employees. It also suggests incompetent hiring procedures resulting in bringing in unqualified people and those with personality problems who make the workplace uncomfortable for coworkers.

Turnover statistics for larger companies can be found in reference reports in your local library. News reports on large layoffs can also be found there or on the Internet. For those positions that are advertised, you can check out how many times in the last year the ad has been placed in the publication where you found it.

A company's layoff history can also be researched. Layoffs are sometimes unavoidable because of economic downturns or contract duration. Some industries, such as aircraft manufacturers, are more prone to layoffs than others because of their reliance on short-term contracts. High probability of a layoff within such an industry is often offset by higher pay scales than in other industries.

Nevertheless, frequent layoffs are a useful indicator of employer attitudes concerning the expendability of its workers as well as its commitment to their job satisfaction and well-being. Such firms are less likely to care about providing a worker-friendly environment or institute worker-friendly policies.

Intuition is your best ally in nosing out management attitudes toward staff. During your visit to the facility, your sense of the place and the people you encounter may suggest appropriate questions and also give you a lot of answers you need. How comfortable are you with what you observe? Do you find yourself uneasy? Are there overtones and offhand comments which suggest possible problems for you?

Facilities often provide clues to the attitude of management toward workers. Such factors as poor lighting, dingy quarters, crowding and lack of privacy speak of an "us against them" management philosophy. While not every employer has sufficient funds to provide you with the latest in technology, those tools you do need should be present and in good working order.

> ### *HIGH IMPACT TIP*
> Assessing company policies toward employees is best carried out in discrete fashion. Expression of overly open concern about possible restrictive policies during an interview suggests an employee more interested in what she can get away with than in what she can produce

There's no simple easily laid out method of determining precisely what unspecified company policies actually are. They're unlikely to appear in its policy handbook. Few firms which engage in the practice, for example, state outright that an employee found to be looking for another job is automatically fired.

Intuition may be your only indicator that a firm has policies that are wrong for you. A sense that something's amiss should lead you to look further at those policies and the firm's history. You might ask discrete questions of the employer himself to determine his attitudes toward and goals for employees.

Other possibilities for **Qualifying** employer attitudes toward workers are making discrete inquiries to present or past employees and others in the community where the firm is located. Often, firms with poor employee relations gain a reputation for that within the community.

**Qualifying** a company cannot absolutely guarantee that your next employer or your next workplace environment will fully meet your requirements. Still, by taking time to consider and research the question and basing your decision on solid information, you greatly increase the odds of having that happen.

# THAT ALL-IMPORTANT INTERVIEW

You've finally arrived! You've finally achieved the result you've been directing such intense efforts toward from the beginning right up into this culminating moment in your job search. Now at an employer's invitation, you've set a mutually convenient date and time for an interview. Now what?

At this point, the typical job seeker has an attack of pre-interview jitters. "What is he going to ask me?" "What am I going to say?" "Will I say the wrong thing?"

As a *TAKE-CHARGE Career Manager*, you're primed and ready to talk to your next employer. By following the *TAKE-CHARGE Strategies* laid out in these chapters, you've been preparing for interviewing employers right from the beginning.

> You've looked closely at the category of job you truly want and elements of the environment you work best in so that you know precisely what you are seeking.

> You've enumerated your skills to support your choice and qualify you for the position offered.

> You've determined, listed and described relevant elements of your work experience and education supporting your candidacy.

> You've listed personal qualities enabling you to fulfill requirements of the job and be productive in it.

> You've **qualified** the employer to have an appreciation of her needs and ideas about how you can help solve her problems–which led to this interview.

Each item above and all of them together give you plenty to talk about with any prospective employer in terms she can relate to. You've taken the time to do the preparatory work. Now you can approach your interview with confidence because you have a story to tell, facts to back it up and words to express it.

A good sales specialist knows his product's selling points. He spends time with a client finding out what her needs are and pointing out how his product's selling points meet them. Once she is convinced, he brings up conditions of the sale as part of the negotiations to close the deal.

> **Qualifying** the employer enabled you to determine this employer's needs in part. You can further explore them in the interview.

> Your experience, education, expertise and personal qualities are your selling points. You can profitably spend the bulk of your interview showing how these meet her identified needs.

> Your career and environmental preferences together with her requirements are the condition of the sale.

---

### HIGH-IMPACT TIP

First impressions are lasting impressions. You won't get a second chance to make a good first impression! An interviewer's first impression of you only too often makes or breaks your chances with this firm!

Show respect for your prospective employer and your future job by dressing and acting appropriately for the occasion. In today's casual world, good grooming, neatness, cleanliness and good manners will put you miles ahead of your competition with many employers right from the start.

Proper dress is particularly important for young job seekers not long out of school. A casual attitude toward dress and poor manners say strongly that you don't give a damn about the job, the employer, coworkers or clients.

Business attire seldom makes the wrong impression. For factory or day labor jobs, cleaned pressed work clothes are appropriate.

---

# The application form

When you walk into an interviewer's door, you'll be handed an application form and asked to fill it out as the first item of business. You will be required to fill one out even though you provided a resume. Once in a great while, you may have already received such a form in the mail along with a request for or confirmation of an interview. In that case, it is accompanied by a request to bring it already filled out to your interview.

Employers use application forms for several purposes. The most obvious is to get your vital statistics on record should you be hired. The more likely that you are in the small group of preferred candidates, the more likely your application form will be scrutinized with great care.

Application forms are used as an additional screening device to *disqualify* candidates for a position. One criterion is truthfulness. At times, information selectively left out of a resume shows up on an application form.

Other discrepancies show up there as well. Examples are long periods of unemployment or multiple jobs over a short period of time. These suggest possible non-employability because of severe personality, motivation or behavior problems.

Many an interviewer uses the form to aid in discussion with you. She may ask questions to flesh out what you've said there and in your resume or cover letter. She will certainly draw inferences about your personality and drive from your answers.

In filling out the form, give requested information as completely as you can. However, you need not necessarily fill in every blank. The **TAKE-CHARGE *Career Manager*** uses discretion in his responses to make sure that what he says here is consistent with what's said in his resume. He is ready with an explanation for any discrepancies.

You need not list every job you ever held, just those relevant to the job you're seeking. This depends somewhat on the stage of your career. Jobs held while in high school are important for an entry-level position and irrelevant later on.

> ### *HIGH-IMPACT TIP*
> Assume that former employers *will be contacted* if possible to verify information you have provided on an application form or in a resume, especially if you are being seriously considered for a position.
>
> If you had difficulties with a supervisor in a previous job and must list the job because you gained significant experience or expertise in it, use the name of someone who is sympathetic to you with that person's permission as your contact person within that firm. See ***Oh! Oh! You were fired! What to do! What to do!*** In SECTION B for further tips.
>
> When your employment is being seriously considered, any dates you provide will be verified. For legal reasons, many large employers do not give any information beyond verifying that you were employed there and your dates of employment.

Character references will not be checked except in extraordinary circumstances. As one personnel management consultant remarked, "Anyone who cannot come up with three friends who will vouch for him is a sad case indeed!"

Applications for higher management positions are often far more extensive. Expect them to explore motivation in much greater depth.

If you are asked to answer questions extensively in longhand, it's very likely that your handwriting will be analyzed. Many large and smaller companies use this service. There is no other valid reason for such a request. You give implicit permission for the analysis in your application.

The very best counsel of this expert graphologist is that you have nothing to fear from such an analysis. Use your ordinary handwriting without attempting to change it. Attempts to change handwriting degrades the sample from the analyst's point of view and may make you seem less intelligent than you actually are. You may also inadvertently introduce other negative factors. The analyst is not looking for what you may think he is.

## Three kinds of interview

An employment interview is an extended conversation between an employer or her representative and a job applicant for the purpose of determining whether a fit exists between an employer with her needs and requirements and an applicant with his experience, expertise and aspirations.

In larger operations, especially for professional or management positions and key clerical jobs, you may undergo as many as four interviews before a hiring decision is made. Disqualification may come at any stage of the process. You will be thanked for applying and dismissed.

The first is a screening interview to weed out obvious misfits. You may not even be aware that you are being evaluated. That innocuous looking receptionist who hands you an application blank may actually be a screener trained to ask certain questions and to assess your behavior in the waiting room. Be sure to treat her as you do any other interviewer.

The second interview is with a hiring specialist from personnel. This interview usually focuses on fleshing out your attitude, motivation, education and employment history. A major objective is to weed out misfits.

Subsequent interviews are with line managers and key professionals who will directly interact with you or supervise your activities should you be hired. These focus on the depth of your technical knowledge, but also assess the probable chemistry of your personal interactions with them.

## Negotiating your interview

Interviewing is a two-way street with interests of both parties at stake. Ideally, an interview ought to balance interests of applicant and employer so common ground can be reached as a basis for future collaboration satisfying both parties.

As a **TAKE-CHARGE Career Manager**, keep in mind while interviewing that your interests are fully as important and deserve as much attention during the interview as those of the firm. Recognizing that as fact enables you to negotiate as an equal partner for both the job and conditions that you truly want.

Generally, the interviewer representing the employer leads the interview and controls its flow and direction. It is important to respect and defer to that lead. Still, an applicant can certainly discretely influence the flow and direction of conversation both by appropriate responses to the interviewer and by raising pertinent questions.

Most, though not all, interviewers have had some training in effective interview techniques or learned them through experience of many interviews. Expect your interviewer to read between the lines of what you say and do during your conversation in order to draw inferences about your attitude. Sound preparation will help you negotiate most pitfalls.

As you enter the room, your interviewer will attempt to set you at ease with a greeting and invite you to be seated. Return his greeting and shake his hand firmly if it is offered before sitting down where he indicates. Don't sit until invited to do so.

Some conduct interviews over a desk, a symbol of authority. Others prefer a more casual seating arrangement in order to disarm you with a symbol of a level playing field. It's fair to draw inferences from these and other choices.

Either way, defer to his leadership of the discussion. Sit at moderate attention without slouching or sprawling. Don't place any object on his desk without explicit permission.

Answer questions fully but briefly and as directly, forthrightly and positively as possible without straying from fact or distorting the record. Look directly at the interviewer while speaking to him.

An interviewer usually has a sequence of questions in mind, sometimes from a programmed list. He deviates from it in order to explore areas suggested by your responses and questions. His foremost task is to investigate your attitudes toward work, employers and fellow employees in order to judge whether you fit into his operation and will stay on the job long enough to justify the expense of being hired.

His second task is to determine if your capabilities fit the job being offered.

Correspondingly, *your foremost task is to convince him that you have positive attitudes toward all three and consequently, are likely to become a positive force within his organization and a productive contributor toward realizing its goals!*

While the interviewer is qualifying you for employment, as a **TAKE-CHARGE Career Manager**, you are completing the task of qualifying the employer: You continue to evaluate if the job fits your skills and interests, if this workplace provides an appropriate environment and conditions of employment, and if you are comfortable with the personalities with which you will interact on the job.

Often, he presents information about the company, its goals and the job for which you are being considered at the beginning of the interview. If he does not touch on the subject, it's well worth your while to get as full a statement from him as he will give of what those goals might be. Doing so will aid the process of qualifying.

For professional positions, such as teaching, check to make sure that the professional philosophy and approach of the firm or institution interviewing you is in sync with your ideas. This reduces the probability that professional disagreements will come up during your tenure leading to dissatisfaction on both sides.

Be as positive as you can be in your responses to questions. Some seemingly routine questions trip up many applicants and end their chances of employment.

For example, while reviewing your resume, the interviewer very casually will ask, "Why did you leave that company?" Your response gives him quite a lot of useful information about your attitudes. Only too many applicants use this to launch into a lengthy criticism of former employers, bosses, or colleagues.

Everything you say about a former employer may be true. This just isn't the appropriate time or place to air such feelings or information. Instead of getting the sympathy you seek, complaints peg you as a potential malcontent. Better to get rid of you *now* before investing company funds in you than have to do so later on after a history of unwanted problems.

Place the most positive construction you can muster on circumstances under which you left a former employer and your reasons for leaving. Among responses most employers will find acceptable to this question are:

- "I saw an opportunity to advance my career significantly beyond what seemed to be available to me at that firm."

- "I launched a new career at that time and moved to a position where I could pursue it."

- "I left to return to school."

- "I was laid off because (choose one or more appropriately) the company downsized or was bought out or ended a major contract or relocated or went out of business."

- "My spouse was transferred or found a job in another location. We decided to relocate our family."

- "I had to take care of an urgent family situation (such as a new baby or a family member's serious illness) which no longer needs my constant attention."

Also place the most positive construction you can on anything else that comes up about what may have happened in former periods of employment. This isn't the place to discuss disagreements within your former company. Besides being labeled as a malcontent, questions about your ability to maintain confidentiality may arise.

Currently, there is little reason to worry about what former employers may say about you. Employers seldom give out such information because of legal considerations.

# Negotiating terms of employment

At some point in the discussion, you've responded to all of the interviewer's questions and he to yours. You're satisfied that the exchange of information is complete. You sense a match between the interviewer's interest in you and yours in his firm. At this point, either party may begin negotiations for the terms of employment.

Now is the time to look at salary and benefit packages associated with the job and any other conditions of employment. It is the time to state your own salary requirements. It is also the time to negotiate for other conditions of employment that are important to you.

To make the most of salary and benefits negotiation, it's a good idea to go in with some idea of your market value. A trip to the reference department of your local library or the Internet may yield information about the range of salaries of your line of work on a regional and national basis. Salary ranges paid for various positions by the larger corporations may also be found there. This information gives you an idea of whether you are keeping up with your field in salary, what a specific company is likely to pay and a competitive level at which to place your requirements.

Women particularly are well advised to arm yourselves with information to prevent being paid much less for equal work than your male counterparts.

Some salaries are set by union contract and cannot be negotiated, or, if they can, only within a narrow range. Some jobs are offered at minimum wage level and are not amenable to negotiation. Then, too, some individuals have established a high market value for their services and already know how to compete for top dollar jobs.

It is generally better to set salary requirements somewhat too high than too low, realizing that the company may negotiate you down. If you ask for a below-average salary, your new employer will be happy to give it to you without further discussion.

Your own salary history should also be taken into account. Except under extraordinary circumstances, there is no need to accept a lower salary than you received in your last job.

As a **TAKE-CHARGE Career Manager**, you most probably can set your salary requirement somewhat higher than other applicants. You have used an approach explicitly designed to convince employers of the value of your services right from the start. The time and care you put into preparation and research is about to pay off!

www.ingramcontent.com/pod-product-compliance
Lightning Source LLC
LaVergne TN
LVHW081552060526
838201LV00054B/1879